T0209454

An Analysis of

Ludwig von Mises's

The Theory of Money and Credit

Pádraig Belton

Published by Macat International Ltd
24:13 Coda Centre, 189 Munster Road, London SW6 6AW.

Distributed exclusively by Routledge
2 Park Square, Milton Park, Abingdon, Oxon OX14 4RN
711 Third Avenue, New York, NY 10017, USA

Routledge is an imprint of the Taylor & Francis Group, an informa business

www.macat.com
info@macat.com

Cataloguing in Publication Data
A catalogue record for this book is available from the British Library.
Library of Congress Cataloguing-in-Publication Data is available upon request.
Cover illustration: Jonathan Edwards

ISBN 978-1-912304-01-1 (hardback)
ISBN 978-1-912284-72-6 (paperback)
ISBN 978-1-912284-86-3 (e-book)

Notice
The information in this book is designed to orientate readers of the work under analysis,
to elucidate and contextualise its key ideas and themes, and to aid in the development
of critical thinking skills. It is not meant to be used, nor should it be used, as a
substitute for original thinking or in place of original writing or research. References and
notes are provided for informational purposes and their presence does not constitute
endorsement of the information or opinions therein. This book is presented solely for
educational purposes. It is sold on the understanding that the publisher is not engaged
to provide any scholarly advice. The publisher has made every effort to ensure that
this book is accurate and up-to-date, but makes no warranties or representations with
regard to the completeness or reliability of the information it contains. The information
and the opinions provided herein are not guaranteed or warranted to produce particular
results and may not be suitable for students of every ability. The publisher shall not be
liable for any loss, damage or disruption arising from any errors or omissions, or from
the use of this book, including, but not limited to, special, incidental, consequential or
other damages caused, or alleged to have been caused, directly or indirectly, by the
information contained within.

CONTENTS

THE MACAT LIBRARY

The Macat Library is a series of unique academic explorations of seminal works in the humanities and social sciences – books and papers that have had a significant and widely recognised impact on their disciplines. It has been created to serve as much more than just a summary of what lies between the covers of a great book. It illuminates and explores the influences on, ideas of, and impact of that book. Our goal is to offer a learning resource that encourages critical thinking and fosters a better, deeper understanding of important ideas.

Each publication is divided into three Sections: Influences, Ideas, and Impact. Each Section has four Modules. These explore every important facet of the work, and the responses to it.

This Section-Module structure makes a Macat Library book easy to use, but it has another important feature. Because each Macat book is written to the same format, it is possible (and encouraged!) to cross-reference multiple Macat books along the same lines of inquiry or research. This allows the reader to open up interesting interdisciplinary pathways.

To further aid your reading, lists of glossary terms and people mentioned are included at the end of this book (these are indicated by an asterisk [*] throughout) – as well as a list of works cited.

Macat has worked with the University of Cambridge to identify the elements of critical thinking and understand the ways in which six different skills combine to enable effective thinking.
Three allow us to fully understand a problem; three more give us the tools to solve it. Together, these six skills make up the **PACIER** model of critical thinking. They are:

ANALYSIS – understanding how an argument is built
EVALUATION – exploring the strengths and weaknesses of an argument
INTERPRETATION – understanding issues of meaning

CREATIVE THINKING – coming up with new ideas and fresh connections
PROBLEM-SOLVING – producing strong solutions
REASONING – creating strong arguments

To find out more, visit **WWW.MACAT.COM.**

CRITICAL THINKING AND *THE THEORY OF MONEY AND CREDIT*

Primary critical thinking skill: REASONING
Secondary critical thinking skill: EVALUATION

Ludwig von Mises is an outstanding example of a thinker at work, carefully setting out a tight initial definition of his subject, then evaluating the logical implications of his definition, and finally producing a persuasive, reasoned case for a radical revision of economic policy.

In *The Theory of Money and Credit*, Mises begins by defining what money is, and how it comes to exist. He skeptically examines the received opinion that governments create money, and instead reasons that money comes into existence naturally to solve problems which arise from bartering.

Moving on from this initial definition of money as primarily a medium of exchange, Mises critiques the nearly universal practice of banks only keeping reserves equating to a fraction of their liabilities. His counter-argument is that this irresponsible expansion of the money supply, confusing money substitutes with real money, is responsible for the tendency of most economies to lapse into disastrous "boom" and "bust" cycles. Excessively expanded money supply will lead to poor decisions in investment and speculative bubbles in the prices of assets, he reasons.

Mises also evaluates the work of his predecessors within the Austrian School of economics, such as Carl Menger, judging it to be promising thanks to the introduction of new conceptual tools such as marginal utility, but suggesting that the lack of a strong definition of money is a significant inadequacy. Money, he says, is not fully worked into their systems. Mises reasons that the same tools of marginal utility can be applied to money itself, producing a coherent theory of economics.

This strong emphasis on evaluation reasoning is a defining feature of Mises's work.

ABOUT THE AUTHOR OF THE ORIGINAL WORK

The Austrian and American economist **Ludwig von Mises** was one of the twentieth century's most influential economists, contributing greatly to understanding of the nature of money and the role of margins in making economic decisions. He wrote 25 books, including *The Theory of Money and Credit*, his most important, and had extremely strong influence on mainstream economic thinking that now is taken for granted in university and government departments everywhere.

ABOUT THE AUTHOR OF THE ANALYSIS

Pádraig Belton was educated at Yale, Oxford, and the School of Oriental and African Studies. He has received a Fulbright fellowship and the Royal United Services Institute's Trench-Gascoigne Prize for writing in foreign affairs. A journalist, he contributes for the BBC, *Times Literary Supplement, Spectator,* and S&P's financial newswire.

ABOUT MACAT

GREAT WORKS FOR CRITICAL THINKING

Macat is focused on making the ideas of the world's great thinkers accessible and comprehensible to everybody, everywhere, in ways that promote the development of enhanced critical thinking skills.

It works with leading academics from the world's top universities to produce new analyses that focus on the ideas and the impact of the most influential works ever written across a wide variety of academic disciplines. Each of the works that sit at the heart of its growing library is an enduring example of great thinking. But by setting them in context – and looking at the influences that shaped their authors, as well as the responses they provoked – Macat encourages readers to look at these classics and game-changers with fresh eyes. Readers learn to think, engage and challenge their ideas, rather than simply accepting them.

'Macat offers an amazing first-of-its-kind tool for interdisciplinary learning and research. Its focus on works that transformed their disciplines and its rigorous approach, drawing on the world's leading experts and educational institutions, opens up a world-class education to anyone.'

Andreas Schleicher
Director for Education and Skills, Organisation for Economic
Co-operation and Development

'Macat is taking on some of the major challenges in university education ... They have drawn together a strong team of active academics who are producing teaching materials that are novel in the breadth of their approach.'

Prof Lord Broers,
former Vice-Chancellor of the University of Cambridge

'The Macat vision is exceptionally exciting. It focuses upon new modes of learning which analyse and explain seminal texts which have profoundly influenced world thinking and so social and economic development. It promotes the kind of critical thinking which is essential for any society and economy. This is the learning of the future.'

Rt Hon Charles Clarke, former UK Secretary of State for Education

'The Macat analyses provide immediate access to the critical conversation surrounding the books that have shaped their respective discipline, which will make them an invaluable resource to all of those, students and teachers, working in the field.'

Professor William Tronzo, University of California at San Diego

WAYS IN TO THE TEXT

KEY POINTS

- The Austrian-American academic Ludwig von Mises was born in 1881 in Lviv, then part of Austria-Hungary. Being Jewish, he fled to New York in 1940 and was a visiting professor at New York University until he retired in 1969.

- For Mises, money is solely a common medium of exchange, and government should interfere as little as possible in determining its value.

- Mises's arguments were central in the foundation of the influential Austrian School of economics, which contributed many of the formative concepts to mainstream economics today.

Who Was Ludwig von Mises?

Born in 1881 in what is now the Ukrainian city of Lviv, and was then the Austro-Hungarian city of Lamberg, Ludwig Edler von Mises grew up there and in Vienna, in a Jewish family which had been raised to the lower aristocracy by Emperor Franz Josef.* His father Arthur was a highly trained engineer, and took a leading position in the Ministry for Railways overseeing construction of railroads; his mother was the niece of a Liberal Party deputy in Austria's parliament.[1] Aged twelve, Mises could speak German, Polish, and French fluently, read Latin, and understand Ukrainian. He studied law at the University of Vienna, receiving a doctorate in 1906.

In his early years Mises worked, variously, at a Vienna law firm, as an economics lecturer, an economic adviser to several politicians and chambers of commerce, as an artillery officer, and as economic adviser to the Austro-Hungarian War Department during the First World War.[*2]

In 1934, as Nazism* rose in neighboring Germany, Mises left Vienna to work as a professor in Geneva's Graduate Institute of International Studies. In 1940, he left Europe and settled in New York City, where he would remain the rest of his life. Supported by a series of foundations, he held a position as an unsalaried visiting professor at New York University from 1945 until he retired in 1969.

In his writing as well as his lecturing—which included seminars in formal university settings as well as ones given at his apartment—Mises developed the concepts of classical liberalism,* while emphasizing choice and purposeful behavior in his idea of praxeology.* His writings have influenced mainstream economics,* but, like much of the Austrian School* in the later twentieth century, they largely sit outside it because of their rejection of modeling and mathematics.

Altogether Mises wrote 25 books, of which *The Theory of Money and Credit* in 1912 was the first, containing the seeds of much of the rest of his thought. He also enlarged it with a new fourth section in an English-language edition in 1953.

Mises died, in 1973, aged 92.

What Does *The Theory of Money and Credit* Say?
Mises's book *The Theory of Money and Credit* presents an argument for how money came to exist. Money, it says, would not be necessary in a world of self-sufficient households, or a centrally planned economy. It similarly is not necessary in a society based on a division of labor* that is based on direct exchange, or bartering.*

However, in a world in which individuals trade many goods, they come to need a medium of exchange: bartering horses for telescopes requires an exact alignment between one person (who has horses, and desires telescopes) and a second person (who has telescopes, but would rather have horses). This can be thought of as a double coincidence of wants. But what if a telescope is worth one and a half horses?

As division of labor becomes more specialized, then there will be a demand on the part of everyone who participates in the primitive economy for something to use as a common medium of exchange.*

Grains of wheat might be a means of exchange, since wheat is a commonly needed good, and so someone selling it normally will be able to find a market. With wheat as a medium of exchange, it is possible to separate the horse-telescope barter into two exchanges: someone who has a telescope and someone who would like to buy it; and similarly, a seller and a buyer of a horse.

Grains of wheat, however, are difficult to transport, and so if the market of money includes wheat, brass, and silver, individuals will wish to trade their goods for the most broadly used means of exchange, which will drive out the others.

For Mises, this function of money as a common medium of exchange is not only its primary, but also its sole function. He argues that other functions of money, such as facilitating credit, follow directly from this one.

Based on his argument that money is solely a common medium of exchange, Mises derives other prescriptions, including the role of government. He suggests that government should protect contracts through courts, and not interfere with the value of money (for instance, by encouraging inflationary or deflationary monetary policy.*) Money derives from voluntary social cooperation, not from the dictates of a government.

Why Does *The Theory of Money and Credit* Matter?

It is hard to overstate the importance of *The Theory of Money and Credit*, a contribution for which Mises has been described as "one of the leading European economists of his time."[3]

At a time when John Maynard Keynes* was convincing governments to engage in deficit spending and helping to create modern macroeconomics* theory with his idea of the business cycle,* Mises offered a sharply contrasting view focused on the usefulness of money as a means of exchange.

Mises's views in *The Theory of Money and Credit* were foundational in the creation of an influential tradition in economics that came to be known as the Austrian School.* In its early decades, the Austrian School rebelled against a more historical approach in economics scholarship which particularly dominated in German-speaking countries. Members of the Austrian school instead sought to emphasize the logical processes that lay behind these historical case studies.

As time progressed, Mises and the Austrian School contributed a number of extremely important concepts which now lie at the heart of mainstream economics. The influential ideas of Mises and other Austrian School scholars include the idea of marginal utility.* This is the change in utility* (that is, happiness, well-being, or satisfaction) achieved by the last unit of a good or service that a person consumes. Closely related to marginal utility is the idea of diminishing marginal utility: that the first unit of a good or service yields greater results than subsequent ones.

The Austrian School split shortly after the Second World War.* One part, represented by Friedrich Hayek,* continued to operate within the mainstream tradition of neoclassical economics, while still being largely skeptical of government intervention. A second tradition, of which Mises forms a part, rejected much of contemporary mainstream economics as flawed, in particular its emphasis on mathematics, macroeconomics,* and modeling.* Its influence is currently strongest amongst libertarians*, particularly in the United States.

The later split aside however, Mises's concepts of marginalism,* subjective value,* and money as a medium of exchange as expressed in *The Theory of Money and Credit* will help readers understand some of the most important concepts in contemporary mainstream economics, and how they arose, in a new, illuminating way.

Over a century after its initial publication, *The Theory of Money and Credit* remains indispensable reading for anyone interested in understanding the nature of money and the origin of some of the most important principles in mainstream economics today. Among the awards that Mises received after writing the book were the Austrian Decoration for Science and Art for political economy, which he received in 1962. A Ludwig von Mises Institute for Austrian Economics exists in Alabama to further his legacy, publishing a *Quarterly Journal of Austrian Economics* as well as a quarterly *Mises Review*.

NOTES

1   Jörg Guido Hülsmann, *Mises: The Last Knight of Liberalism*, Ludwig von Mises Institute, 2007, 9

2   Hülsmann, *Mises*, 286.

3   Richard Ebeling, "The Life and Works of Ludwig Von Mises," *The Independent Review*, 13.1, Summer 2008: 101.

THE AUTHOR AND THE HISTORICAL CONTEXT

KEY POINTS

- *The Theory of Money and Credit* ushers in a new era of economic thought, still relevant today, by integrating Mises's strongly argued theory of money into a general theory of price and marginal utility.

- The Austrian School which Mises represents sought to uncover universal generalizations underneath historical detail and was generally laissez-faire.*

- Mises said that Carl Menger's* *Principles of Economics* "made an 'economist' of me," by converting him to the outlook of the Austrian School outlook.

Why Read This Text?

The impact of Ludwig von Mises's *The Theory of Money and Credit* on how we understand money, the money supply, and other issues in economics, is profound. One economics professor called Mises "the last knight of liberalism" for his devotion to individual choice in an era in which the pendulum tilted toward central planning in free-market as well as socialist countries.[1]

For those familiar with today's mainstream economics, reading *The Theory of Money and Credit* offers insights into the origins of many familiar economic concepts as well as critiques of the direction economic policy and economics have taken since the book was published. Mises's theory of money is significant, but so is how he integrates it into a general theory of marginal utility and price.

> **❝** Mises's great achievement in his *Theory of Money and Credit* was in liberating us from the veil-of-money myth. Money is a commodity by its very nature, not just by historical accident. By realizing this, Mises was in a position to integrate the theory of money into the general framework of marginal-value theory. **❞**
>
> Jörg Guido Hülsmann, *Mises: The Last Knight of Liberalism* (2007)

For those just beginning in economics, reading Mises offers the chance to look at how concepts such as marginal utility, the subjective theory of value, and the theory of money first evolved, in intellectual struggles between Mises and his sparring partners—German economic historians* and, later, Keynesians.*

For those interested in contemporary politics, the divide between libertarians like Mises and more centralizing traditions cuts across both the left and right. Both left-libertarians and right-libertarians are skeptical of the state, preferring voluntary cooperation to centralized planning. (Right-libertarians prefer the market; left-libertarians prefer trade unions or workers' self-management of the workplace, combined with decentralized political organization.)

Mises is not only of historical interest, however. In the wake of the 2008 global financial crisis,* when most governments adopted Keynesian fiscal stimulus with deficit spending, the *Economist* pointed out policymakers took an odd lack of interest in Mises's argument these policies would just add fuel to boom-bust cycles. 'Given the repeated credit booms and busts of the past 40 years, that may be a pity,' the newspaper concluded.[2]

Mises and his arguments remain thus remain enduringly relevant today.

Author's Life

Ludwig von Mises was born on September 29, 1881 in today's Lviv, a city which is now in Ukraine, but was then part of the Austro-Hungarian Empire.* His great-grandfather, the financier, city councilman, and orphanage founder Meyer Rachmiel Mises,* was ennobled that April by Emperor Franz Josef, part of a policy of liberalization toward the empire's Jews. Ludwig's father, Arthur, was a senior engineer for the Czernowitz railroad company, while his maternal uncle, Hermann Mises, was a Liberal member of parliament in 1873 for the county of Drohobycz,* and also a journalist.

When his railroad line was nationalized (around autumn 1887), Arthur von Mises moved his family to Vienna to take up a new post as a civil servant and construction counselor to the railroad ministry. Ludwig and his brothers Richard (later a prominent mathematician) and Karl received excellent educations in the cosmopolitan capital of the Habsburg Empire.* In Ludwig's case, this was at the Akademische Gymnasium,* one of Vienna's best schools and an institution preferred by the liberal bourgeoisie.

In autumn 1900, Mises entered the Department of Law and Government Science at the University of Vienna, where in addition to the four years required to quality for legal practice, he completed three additional examinations for a doctorate. He participated in seminars organized by Carl Grünberg,* against whose historicist approach he later rebelled. Mises's first published research, a 1902 study of government reforms concerning peasant farmers in Galicia,* was completed under Grünberg.

Mises's interest in the theory of money was stimulated by attending lectures given by Friedrich von Wieser,* the University of Vienna's professor of political economy from 1903. So did the work of Wieser's predecessor Carl Menger,* whose *Principles* Mises read around Christmas 1903. Both men were opponents of historicism, making the case for a universal rational economic theory to understand dynamics underlying historical narratives. This approach came to be known as the Austrian School, and the debate between these scholars and the historicists was called the *Methodenstreit*, the great dispute on method.

Reading Menger changed Mises's outlook, seeing the free market instead of government intervention as offering human betterment. By February 1906, he gained the title of *doctor juris utriusque* (doctor of canon and secular law), and began to attend the seminars of Eugen Böhm-Bawerk,* a four-time Minister of Finance under whose guidance Mises began researching money and banking.

Mises wrote his first books (*The Theory of Money and Credit* in 1912, with five more by 1933) while working for several public clients as an economic adviser, before the 1934 assassination of Austria's Chancellor by local Nazis cast his country's future in doubt.

Mises spent six years in Switzerland as a professor at Geneva's Institut des Hautes Études Internationales (Graduate Institute of International Studies), before moving to New York in 1940. There, supported by the Rockefeller and Volker Foundations and with private assistance from the journalist and advertising executive Lawrence Fertig,* he worked as a visiting professor at New York University from 1945 until his retirement in 1969, four years before his death at the age of 92.

Author's Background

Mises's work in *The Theory of Money and Credit* arises out of the quarrel of the first members of the Austrian School with the then-dominant historical school of economics.

Carl Menger's* *Principles of Economics*, published in 1871, launched the Austrian School, and with it its struggle (*Methodenstreit*) with the Historical School* and its leading representative Gustav von Schmoller.* Schmoller, who from 1899 represented the University of Berlin in the Prussian House of Lords, coined the term 'Austrian School' to paint his opponents as provincials from sleepy Austria instead of scholars from the self-confident German Empire.* But *Kathedersozialismus** ("[University] Chaired Socialists")—the term coined by the Austrian School to describe its enemies, many of whom were prominent advocates of the idea of the welfare state—also stuck.

Menger rejected the labor theory of value* used by Adam Smith* to explain the value of goods (and still employed by Marxist* economists). In its place, Menger introduced the concept of marginal utility. In particular, argued Menger, marginal utility explained the diamond-water paradox which had flummoxed classical economists like Smith.* This was the puzzle of why diamonds were more expensive than water, when water is more important for survival.

Mises later said Menger's *Principles* "made an 'economist' of me," by which he meant a proponent of the superior value of free enterprise and voluntary individual association to grand schemes of the state.[3] Mises perceived this as the tradition of the British classical economists (such as Adam Smith) as well as the leading French économistes (including Henri de Saint-Simon* and Yves Guyot*) of the eighteenth and nineteenth centuries.

NOTES

1   Jörg Guido Hülsmann, *Mises: The Last Knight of Liberalism*, Ludwig von Mises Institute, 2007.

2   'Taking von Mises to Pieces,' *Economist*, November 18, 2010. http://www.economist.com/node/17522368, accessed on December 27, 2017.

3   Mises, *Notes and Recollections*, Indianapolis: Liberty Fund: [1940-1], 2014, 33.

MODULE 2
ACADEMIC CONTEXT

KEY POINTS

- Mises's *The Theory of Money and Credit* was his "habilitation" thesis, prepared after his doctorate to permit him to teach at university level.

- The first members of the Austrian School had begun to explore marginal utility and the nature of money. Mises attempted to further refine their theory of money.

- Marginal utility offered a solution to paradoxes which classical economics could not solve.

The Work In Its Context

Ludwig von Mises's *The Theory of Money and Credit* expands Carl Menger's theory of value and prices by formulating a theory of money and banking, and then integrating it into Menger's framework.

The work began as his postdoctoral thesis which Mises wrote in order to be able to teach at a university. The term for this, in German, is *Habilitationsschrift*.* Many Continental countries, including France and Germany, also require similar 'habilitation' dissertations, after a doctorate, before someone is eligible to be a professor. After Mises completed *The Theory of Money and Credit*, he began working as a *Privatdozent*, an unpaid private lecturer affiliated to the University of Vienna, before being made an associate professor in 1918.

During this busy time for him, he gave seminars, pursued his early research on money and banking, and also headed the finance department for the Vienna Chamber of Commerce and Industry. Despite his junior standing in the university, his seminars, both in his

> **❝** No very deep knowledge of economics is usually needed for grasping the immediate effects of a measure; but the task of economics is to foretell the remoter effects, and so to allow us to avoid such acts as attempt to remedy a present ill by sowing the seeds of a much greater ill for the future. **❞**
>
> Ludwig von Mises, *The Theory of Money and Credit*

private apartment and in his office at the Chamber of Commerce, were extremely well attended. They attracted such regular participants as Friedrich von Hayek, Oskar Morgenstern* (who later, at Princeton, would be one of the founders of game theory*), and Fritz Machlup* (who, later and also as a Princeton professor, is credited with the concept of the information society*). As well as attracting economists within the Austrian School, Mises's seminars drew many members of the Vienna Circle.* This was a thriving group of philosophers, mathematicians, and natural and social scientists who gathered around the logical positivist* Moritz Schlick.* (Ludwig's younger brother, the mathematician Richard von Mises, was a member of Schlick's inner circle.)

At the time he was writing *The Theory of Money and Credit*, Mises also was close friends with the economist and sociologist Max Weber, Mises's elder by 17 years. Their friendship flourished despite Weber's position within the Historical School, and Mises contributed to the highly-regarded *Archiv für Sozialwissenschaften und Sozialpolitik* (the Archive for Social Sciences and Social Policy) which Weber edited. Mises admired Weber's work, as well as his commitment to methodological individualism,* seeking to explain social phenomena by using the motivations and actions of individuals.

Overview Of The Field

Marginal utility presents the value of a thing as subjective—the utility (or happiness or benefit) from consuming the twelfth in a box of doughnuts will not be the same as that derived from the first in the box.

This understanding of value in sharp distinction to Marxist economists, who conceive value as deriving from the labor spent on its production. It also contrasts sharply with classical economists, like Adam Smith and John Law, who explained value strictly in terms of supply and demand, but then had difficulty explaining why diamonds have a higher price than water.

This concept of marginal utility—that the value of a good derives from its *marginal* utility (or demand) and *marginal* cost (or supply)—was, at the time Ludwig von Mises wrote *The Theory of Money and Credit*, being explored simultaneously by at least three economic schools, located in Vienna, Lausanne, and Cambridge. (There also was a smaller Swedish school led by Knut Wicksell* and Erik Lindahl* at the University of Lund.)

The work of Menger, Böhm-Bawerk, and Wieser, all members of the first generation of the Austrian School, identifies the concept of marginal utility. The concept is then developed further by Mises and Hayek, who occasionally were referred to as the younger Austrians.

Very similar work was being done, at roughly the same time, in Switzerland by the Lausanne School* (and economists such as Léon Walras* and Vilfredo Pareto*, who both held the economics chair at the University of Lausanne). This also is true of an Anglo-American* or Cambridge School* (and William Stanley Jevons* at University College London, and Keynes's teacher Alfred Marshall at Cambridge).

The work of the Lausanne and Cambridge Schools was much more heavily mathematical, while the Austrian School preferred verbal argument. Ultimately, though the mathematical approach would prevail in economics over the twentieth century, the Austrian School would prove more influential.

This is in part because many of its members were displaced by the Second World War and took up places afterwards in US universities, helping spread the School's ideas.

Ultimately, the concept of marginal utility would prove the Austrian School's great contribution to the twentieth-century tradition of neo-classical economics. Neo-classical economics, in turn—after absorbing some elements from Keynesianism—has yielded mainstream economics now practiced in most university departments, finance ministries, and international financial institutions today.

Academic Influences

Ludwig von Mises took much from the Austrian School's founder Carl Menger, in both his analysis of money and his methods of exploring marginal utility.

Menger's theory of money, like Mises's, starts with an examination of the nature of money itself. For both Menger and Mises, money is a commodity used in indirect exchanges, and bought and sold primarily to effectuate them. Also, for both of them, money emerges spontaneously to remedy the problem of double coincidence of wants: to continue an analogy from earlier, if you wish to sell a telescope to someone who has a horse, but you do not yourself actually want a horse.

This argument, that money does not come into being by an act of government, or even without a prior social contract, has an eighteenth-century legacy which goes back even before Adam Smith to the Scottish economist John Law.*[1]

Menger's influence on Mises was chiefly indirect, through his writings and pupils, as he resigned his professorship at the University of Vienna in 1903. A second, more personal, influence on Mises was his teacher Eugen Böhm-Bawerk, who had been a student of Menger's, and served as Minister for Finance in four consecutive

Austrian cabinets from 1895 to 1904. He then resigned to accept a post at the University of Vienna, where he taught until his death ten years later.

Böhm-Bawerk's research during his time in Vienna culminated in his essay *Power or Economic Law?*—which argued wages were determined by supply and demand, not by changing power relationships between management and workers. Government intervention, he said, could not rewrite these economic laws. It is an argument very much like those Mises would make throughout his own career.

A third important influence on Mises was Friedrich von Wieser, who was Böhm-Bawerk's brother-in-law. Wieser also was a founding member of the Vienna School, and succeeded Menger in his post at the University of Vienna. Wieser's development of the concept of marginal utility—to which he gave its name (*Grenznutzen*, in his original German)—was an important influence on Mises. Wieser strove to build on Menger's study of the historical evolution of money by adding in considerations of marginal utility. Mises built on this early attempt, and fleshed it out into his complex framework in *The Theory of Money and Credit*.

NOTES

1 Arthur Monroe, *Monetary Theory before Adam Smith*, New York: August Kelley ([1923] 1966).

THE PROBLEM

KEY POINTS

- Mises attempts to apply the ideas of methodological individualism and marginal utility to constructing a framework of rigorous, universally applicable rules in economics.

- He seeks to remedy flaws in the work of preceding members of the Austrian School.

- The concept of marginal utility, as revised by Mises, became the basis of neoclassical economics in the later twentieth century.

Core Question

In *The Theory of Money and Credit*, Ludwig von Mises identified and example of circular thinking in the work of Austrian School founder Carl Menger. For Menger, in his 1871 *Principles of Economics*, money has a value which is determined by supply and demand. The fact it is in demand presupposes, though, that it has a purchasing power. So the conclusion, says Mises, is circular: the argument, for its proof, relies on what it is aiming to prove.

One possible response to Mises's argument is simply to say the purchasing power of money today is derived by today's actors in the market by looking to the purchasing power it had yesterday. Yesterday, they looked at the value it had the day before; and so on. But this answer is not satisfying, either, because it relies on an infinite recursion.* The process has to begin somewhere.

Mises's problem, then, was this: he wished to put forward the basis of a generalizable economics whose rules and principles were founded

> ❝ For the naive mind there is something miraculous in the issuance of fiat money. A magic word spoken by the government creates out of nothing a thing which can be exchanged against any merchandise a man would like to get. How pale is the art of sorcerers, witches, and conjurors when compared with that of the government's Treasury Department! ❞
>
> Ludwig von Mises, *The Theory of Money and Credit*

in logic. To do this, however, meant taking issue with the work of the Historical School, which argued that economic interactions were specific to a time and place, and could only really be understood by rich investigation of particular motives, actions, and their contexts.

Mises also—and in common with the founding members of the Austrian School like Menger, Wieser, and Böhm-Bawerk—wished to put forward a universal theory based on methodological individualism and marginality. Methodological individualism is the requirement that explanations for social phenomena be based on the choices and motivations of individual decision-makers. Marginal utility looks to the additional benefit one *further* unit of a good or service will bring someone, at the point they are purchasing it.

Mises recognized the attractiveness of methodological individualism and marginal utility in grounding an economics based on universally valid logical axioms. At the same time, and for all its promise, he acknowledged that the work of first-generation Austrian School thinkers was incomplete and flawed.

His question, therefore, in *The Theory of Money and Credit*, is this: how can an economics based in universal patterns in the behavior of individuals, explain what money is? That being done, how can we apply the consequences of such a rigorous concept of money to offer reliable truths about credit, banking, and business cycles?

The Participants

Writing 130 years before Mises, Adam Smith described price in terms of supply and demand. However, like many classical economists, he was puzzled by what he described as the diamond–water paradox (also called the paradox of value*). That is, why are diamonds more expensive than water?

As Smith says in 1776 in *The Wealth of Nations*, "nothing is more useful than water: but it will purchase scarce any thing; scarce any thing can be had in exchange for it. A diamond, on the contrary, has scarce any value in use; but a very great quantity of other goods may frequently be had in exchange for it."[1] Smith attempted to answer the dilemma by saying price, as a value in exchange, is a different thing to a value in use. He then proceeds to focus on the first of these, value in exchange.

For Karl Marx, writing *Capital* nearly a century later in 1867, this was a weak answer. Marx seized on flaws in how classical economists saw price to formulate his own labor theory of value. For Smith, the price of a buggy whip has just to do with supply and demand at the point of sale, and not the labor spent creating it. For Marx however, the true value of the buggy whip is *indeed* the amount of time required for a worker (or workers) of average skill and productivity, working with average tools, to produce it. The difference between this value, and the wage workers receive, Marx calls surplus labor.* Capitalists* pocket this, and capitalist markets focus on the commodities themselves, thereby obscuring the deeper social relationships which produce them. Marx calls this commodity fetishism.*

Mises's teachers in the first generation of the Austrian School attempt to provide another answer to the water–diamond paradox, which is closer to Smith's original thought. Carl Menger, writing the *Principles of Economics* in 1871, stressed that people make economic decisions under constraints of uncertainty, and they make these decisions one at a time, about whether to purchase a particular additional unit of a good or service. The source of economic value is thus in the individual's mind—not how much labor went into a commodity, or calculations steeped in perfect knowledge about the whole of supply and demand. This is the approach which Mises explores further, and more systematically, in *The Theory of Money and Credit*.

The Contemporary Debate

From today's perspective, the rise of these ideas of methodological individualism and marginality are the developments that produce neoclassical economics in the twentieth century, from out of the eighteenth and nineteenth century classical economic tradition represented by Smith.

The widespread adoption of the concept of marginal utility within economics has, in fact, been called the Marginal Revolution.*

Marginal utility gives a greater explanatory power to economics rooted in the classical tradition. It also represents a response which Marx's *Capital* (whose first volume appeared in 1867), and economists inspired by him, posed to the classical tradition.

Today, Marxian* economists continue to use Marx's labor theory of value and his concept of surplus labor. Meanwhile, mainstream economists, continuing the neoclassical project, use marginal utility as their most important concept. For them, every rational individual has a utility function, which represents how much utility (or benefit) they expect to derive from different amounts of consumption. However, since individuals always make decisions under constraints of uncertainty, they will try to maximize their expected utility.* A particularly influential way of describing decision-making under uncertainty, which draws from methodological individualism and marginal utility, is the von Neumann-Morgenstern utility theorem.* This was created in 1947 by Hungarian mathematician John von Neumann* jointly with Mises's doctoral student Oskar Morgenstern.

Both Menger and Mises, however, rejected these mainstream mathematical approaches, and the model-building and statistical scholarship these approaches led to. There are some scholars identifying with the Austrian School today who continue to hold this position, such as Jesús Huerta de Soto at the Mises Institute. (Huerta de Soto has described modern economics scholarship bitingly as based on "intersection of mysterious curves or functions lacking any real existence...even in the minds of the actors involved."[2]) However, other contemporary Austrians, such as Steven Horwitz,* an economics professor at Ball State University, have argued Austrian School tenets can be expressed in terms of microeconomic and macroeconomic models.[3]

NOTES

1   Adam Smith, *An Inquiry into the Nature and Causes of the Wealth of Nations*, (London: W. Strahan and T. Cadell, 1776): Book 1, Chapter 4, 34.

2   Jesús Huerta de Soto, *Socialismo, Cálculo Económico y Función Empresarial*. Madrid: Unión Editorial, 1992, 35.

3   Steven Horwitz, *Microfoundations and Macroeconomics: An Austrian Perspective*, London: Routledge: 2000.

MODULE 4
THE AUTHOR'S CONTRIBUTION

KEY POINTS

- Mises aims to bring the Austrian theory of value full circle by showing that money can be fully explained by the theories of marginal utility and subjective value.

- Mises argues that money is good in its own right, not just a placeholder for other goods.

- He argues against the Keynesian policy of countercyclical deficit spending during recessions because it weakens the value of money.

Author's Aims

When he wrote *The Theory of Money and Credit* in 1912, Ludwig von Mises was 31 and a young academic. It was the first step a series of great systematizing projects of economics research on which he spent the remainder of his writing life.

Publication of the book established his academic reputation and secured him a teaching position at the University of Vienna, where Mises worked his theory of money and banking into the framework his teacher, Carl Menger, had established to examine value and prices. Mises thereby continued an Austrian School tradition of beginning his career with an analysis of money. Menger's theory of money, which formed chapter 8 of his *Principles*, was his own *Habilitationsschrift* as a young researcher.

Menger's *Principles* developed the theory of marginal value, one of the key contributions of the Austrian School to economics in the twentieth century. Money itself he treats as a social institution, and he gives some thought to how it grows out of a non-monetary

> **"** Economic affairs cannot be kept going by magistrates and policemen. **"**
>
> Ludwig von Mises, *The Theory of Money and Credit*

commodity. However, Menger did not apply his own theory of marginal value to money itself. This left the impression that money was not subject to the same rules as value theory. For Menger, it seems, value theory only applied to consumer goods and the means of production.[1]

Mises's aim in *The Theory of Money and Credit* was therefore to bring the Austrian theory of value and prices full circle by showing that money, like all other goods, could be fully brought within the new marginal-value theory and its related concept, the subjective theory of value (the idea that the value of a good is determined by the importance individuals place on it).

Later, in an intellectual autobiography written in 1940 on his arrival in the United States, Mises described his motivations by saying, "The systems of Menger and Böhm-Bawerk were no longer wholly satisfactory to me. I was ready to proceed further on the road these old masters had discovered. But I could not use their treatment of those problems with which monetary theory must begin."[2]

Approach

In *The Theory of Money and Credit*, Mises aimed to extend the theory of marginal value and prices, which had previously so thoroughly transformed economics in the work of the earliest Austrian School authors, to the theory of money itself.

This allowed Mises to argue that money was no longer a special case, but could be fully explained in terms of Austrian thinking about marginal value. "According to prevailing opinion at that time," he explains in his autobiography, "the theory of money could be clearly separated from the total structure of economic problems—it did not, in fact, even belong with economics; in a certain respect it was an independent discipline." [3] For Mises, in contrast, economics must necessarily be "a complete and united whole." [4]

Mises's great insight is that money is a good in its own right. It is not just a placeholder for other goods. For example, if Peter sold a painting, exchanging it for $100, he did so because he perceived he will obtain a greater marginal utility from the $100 than from the painting. Peter values this $100 because of its expected future purchasing power, in permitting him to receive real goods and services with it tomorrow. He expects money to have a certain purchasing power tomorrow, because he has a memory of its purchasing power yesterday—and, yesterday, other people remembered the purchasing power money had the day before. Mises says this regression is not infinite; if you push the explanation back far enough through time, we reach the moment people valued gold or grain for its own sake, and its exchange was a form of barter.

Mises called this the regression theorem.* He argued that it rescues the value of money from accusations of circularity (money has value because people treat it as having value). Using the regression theorem, economists can apply to money the powerful Austrian approaches of marginal utility and the subjective theory of value.

Contribution In Context

For Mises, showing that money's very existence can itself be fully explained by economics is urgent because if it cannot, there is a real danger that monetary policy could become a tool of government. If money comes into existence through the will of states, then states could feel freely able to intervene with its value through inflationary policies and expanding the money supply, he reasons.

Mises is very aware of the *State Theory of Money* by University of Strasbourg economist Georg Friedrich Knapp.* In this book, Knapp argued that the value of money does arise spontaneously through relations of exchange, but instead derives solely from its issuance by an institutional form of government.[5] Knapp founded a school called chartalism,* based on the premise that money is a creature of law, not a commodity.

It is a very short step from Knapp's state theory of money to John Maynard Keynes and his recommendations that states engage in deficit borrowing and spending to balance the business cycle. Keynes argued, in his 1936 *General Theory of Employment, Interest and Money*, that governments should engage in "counter-cyclical" spending to inject money into the economy during times of depression, rectifying insufficient aggregate demand.[6] In fact, the first chapter of Keynes's 1930 *Treatise of Money* begins by drawing heavily from Knapp's work. "Today all civilized money is, beyond the possibility of dispute, chartalist," Keynes says.[7]

In this way, it seems evident that the two great economic approaches of the twentieth century are rooted in two very different understandings of the nature of money. Keynesian economics, with its advocacy of countercyclical deficit spending (i.e., to permit governments to spend their way out of recessions), starts from the perspective that money is something that governments create. In contrast, the approach championed by the Austrian School, that governments can only do harm by interfering with the value of money, draws on Mises's argument that money has a value which arises spontaneously without governments playing any role at all.

NOTES

1   Jörg Guido Hülsmann, *Mises: The Last Knight of Liberalism,* 212.

2   Mises, *Notes and Recollections* (Spring Mills, Pennsylvania: Libertarian Press, 1978), 55.

3   *Notes and Recollections*, 55.

4   *Notes and Recollections*, 55.

5   Georg Friedrich Knapp, *Staatliche Theorie des Geldes* (*State Theory of Money*), London: Macmillan, [1905] 1924.

6   John Maynard Keynes, *The General Theory of Employment, Interest and Money*, London: Palgrave Macmillan, 1936.

7   John Maynard Keynes, *A Treatise of Money*, New York: Harcourt, Brace and Co., 1930. 1/4.

MAIN IDEAS

KEY POINTS

- Mises argues that money is chiefly a means of exchange, and its other purposes follow from this. There are substitutes for money, too, ranging from notes and certificates fully covered by a bank's deposits to "fiduciary media" which are covered only partly, or not at all.

- For Mises, when banks create money, they create artificially low interest rates and credit bubbles, causing people to spend and borrow excessively. The result is a business cycle of destructive booms and busts.

- Mises attempted to write clearly and straightforwardly, seeing the mathematical turn in postwar economics as founded on assumptions he did not accept.

Key Themes

In *The Theory of Money and Credit*, Ludwig von Mises first develops a very persuasive concept of the nature of money. He then proceeds to apply this to better understanding problems about banking and the business cycle.

Mises's analysis of the nature of money, hovering as it does at the center of his work, draws on Menger's. However, Mises expands his teacher's analysis in four important ways.

First, money for Menger was simultaneously a means of exchange, a store of value, a means of immediate or deferred payment, and a measure of value (a *numéraire**). However, Mises observes there is a hierarchy in these functions: that is, a commodity can't really be a store of value if it is not marketable, because people would not be able to release the value contained in a commodity if they could not exchange

> ❝ The excellence of the gold standard is to be seen
> in the fact that it renders the determination of the
> monetary unit's purchasing power independent of the
> policies of governments and political parties. ❞
> Ludwig von Mises, *The Theory of Money and Credit*

that commodity for other things: they would simply be stuck with it. And being a means of exchange is the necessary condition for all the others.

Second, the hierarchy in the functions of money is not Mises's only hierarchy. He also constructs a second, running from money in the narrowest (and best) sense, to all things which *might* be accepted as surrogates for money. These substitutes, issued by banks (like bank deposits and notes), represent legal title to money in the narrow sense.

Third, there is a hierarchy in *these* money substitutes, too. They might be covered by a corresponding amount of money held by the bank, in which case Mises calls them "money certificates."[1] Or they might be only partly (or maybe not at all) covered by money held by the bank. In this last case, Mises calls them fiduciary media* or, in German, *Umlaufsmittel*. (Some translators have simply called this "credit.")

Finally, Mises takes a dim view of fiduciary media. Banks issue money substitutes of this sort to fulfill demand for money, when this is greater than their actual supply of it. In so doing, though, says Mises, they weaken the purchasing power of all money. For Mises, when banks create fiduciary media which are not backed up by money held in their own accounts or vaults, they engage in a very dangerous game indeed.

Exploring The Ideas
Mises's sharp criticism of the current form of banking practiced in

most countries worldwide—fractional-reserve banking,* which is when banks extend loans not fully backed up by their own reserves— has been both powerfully controversial and influential.

This criticism proved the origin of Austrian business cycle theory,* which Friedrich Hayek afterward developed further (in his 1931 *Prices and Production*). Along with a very different approach taken by Keynesian economics, Austrian business cycle theory is one significant influence on how mainstream economics now understands business cycles today.

For Mises, banks creating money (or more precisely, in his terminology, not money but money substitutes, or "fiduciary media") is always a bad idea. In his argument, central banks create credit bubbles* when they lend to private banks, without holding reserves equal to more than a fraction of the loan. Next, private banks themselves make loans, which are not fully backed up either by their reserves or those of the central bank.

The resulting interest rate, for the loan market, is lower than it would be if the money supply were stable. In turn, when interest rates are artificially too low for too long a time, people save less than they otherwise would, and they borrow excessively, leading to speculative "bubbles."* Projects begin to seem profitable which otherwise would not have done, resulting in poor quality investment* and overconsumption.* That is, individuals make investment and consumption decisions which do not reflect the economy's real long-term needs and demands, as these would be expressed with correct price signals in a free market.

This can never end well, says Mises. "There is no means of avoiding the final collapse of a boom brought about by credit expansion," he warns. "The alternative," Mises adds gloomily, "is only whether the crisis should come sooner as a result of the voluntary abandonment of further credit expansion, or later as a final and total catastrophe of the currency system involved."[2]

In this way the distinction between money and fiduciary media, which is at the core of Mises's thinking, leads to one of *The Theory of Money and Credit's* most influential contributions: the way excessively easy credit leads to a business cycle of regularly occurring destructive booms and busts.

Language And Expression

The clarity of Mises's prose, a trait he possibly inherited from his teachers, attracted praise from his very earliest reviewers.[3] His writing has been praised as unique and captivating, as well as precise and careful.

Hayek, Mises's Austrian School contemporary, referred to his clear, well-argued "and deceptively simple prose style."[4] Even Keynes, in later life an antagonist of Mises's, found much to praise in his style of "lucid common sense."[5] Its plainness, however, sometimes hides the breadth and depth of Mises's thought, and sometimes his arguments do not spell out his arguments fully, and tacitly presuppose a good grasp of economic processes from a reader.[6]

At the same time, Mises presents his arguments boldly and unwaveringly, leading some readers to find him more belligerent than other economists.[7] He can be withering, caustic, abrasive, and pungent.

The modern reader is struck by the absence of mathematics from Mises's work. This is not accidental: Mises believed the highly mathematical turn which economics took after the Second World War was based on false assumptions, and so erected a vast and superficially impressive structure on what were, from his perspective, decidedly shaky foundations.

Translating Mises from German to English poses its own problems. Mises published *The Theory of Money and Credit* in Vienna in 1912, with a second edition following in 1924. An English-language translation, by Harold Batson*, an assistant in the economics department at the London School of Economics, did not appear until 1934 from London publishers Jonathan Cape.* The first publishers translated *Umlaufsmittel* as "fiduciary media" in the text, but as "credit" in the title, thinking the more unusual phrase would irritate readers. In 1953, by which time Mises was living in the United States, he produced an expanded English-language edition with Yale University

NOTES

1   Ludwig von Mises, *The Theory of Money and Credit.* Auburn, Alabama: Ludwig von Mises Institute, [1912], 2009, 32-33.

2   Ludwig von Mises, *Human Action: A Treatise on Economics* (*Nationalökonomie: Theorie des Handelns und Wirtschaftens*), Auburn, Alabama: Ludwig von Mises Institute ([1940] 1998), Chapter XX, Section 8, 568.

3   Jörg Guido Hülsmann, *Mises: The Last Knight of Liberalism,* 73.

4   Friedrich Hayek, *The Fortunes of Liberalism: Essays on Austrian Economics and the Ideal of Freedom*, (edited by Peter Klein), Chicago: University of Chicago Press, 1992, 40.

5   John Maynard Keynes, *The Economic Journal*, Vol. 24, No .95 (September 1914), 417.

6   Sudha R. Shenoy, *Towards a Theoretical Framework for British and International Economic History*, Auburn, Alabama: Ludwig von Mises Institute, 2010. 219-301.

7   David Ramsay Steele, *From Marx to Mises: Post-Capitalist Society and the Challenge of Economic Calculation*, La Salle, Illinois: Open Court, 1992, chapter 5.

SECONDARY IDEAS

KEY POINTS

- Money, Mises teaches, does not provide an objective measure of value.

- His ordinal (rank-ordered) view of utility was incorporated into the bases of postwar mainstream economics, influencing approaches like rational choice and game theory.

- An overlooked part of Mises's thinking is the extent to which he has integrated his different influential concepts into a coherent framework.

Other Ideas

Ludwig von Mises's work *The Theory of Money and Credit* is most closely associated with his Regression Theorem, along with his arguments that money is a commodity like any other, and his criticisms of fractional banking. However, Mises's work is ambitious and wide ranging, and he makes a number of other interesting and provocative arguments.

One collection of such arguments revolves around the theory of subjective value. Carl Menger introduces this concept in his *Principles*, saying "value is therefore nothing inherent in goods, no property of them, but merely the importance that we first attribute to the satisfaction of our needs."[1] This is an important contribution which Mises, and the Austrian School, has made to contemporary economics (though subsequent economists use the term "utility" to describe subjective value).

> 66 The advocates of public control cannot do without inflation. They need it in order to finance their policy of reckless spending and of lavishly subsidizing and bribing the voters. 99
>
> Ludwig von Mises, *The Theory of Money and Credit*

Economic value, for the Austrian School, is not a property of goods in themselves, but how individuals judge, at particular moments, those goods will affect their own well-being. By definition, subjective value assumes the possibility that individuals, when they make decisions, will do so based on incomplete information or erroneous judgment.

Mises, however, pushes this idea even further than previous Austrian School authors such as Eugen Böhm-Bawerk and Fredrich von Wieser, who had considered it after Menger. For Mises, subjective evaluations can arrange goods in the order of their significance, for a particular person acting at a particular time. But, he cautions, you cannot measure subjective use-value as a multiple of some unit, or a fraction of the significance of another good.[2] As Mises puts it (here profoundly disagreeing with Böhm-Bawerk's argument), "it is impossible to measure subjective use-value."[3] In other words, while people may prefer an apple to eating six plums, they cannot say the utility (or subjective use-value) of an apple is six times greater than a single plum; the law of decreasing marginal utility holds that the pleasure obtained from the successive plum-units will change. For this reason, says Mises, utility itself cannot be measured: "We may say, the value of this commodity is greater than the value of that; but it is not permissible for us to assert, this commodity is worth *so much* ... this kind of calculation is quite inapplicable to processes of valuation."[4]

Exploring The Ideas

Mises's argument that utility cannot be measured has profound implications. It is meaningful to ask if one option is better than another, he says but it is meaningless to ask how much better, or how good it is in absolute terms.

For Mises, this means utility is ordinal in nature: it can only be ranked. He makes this argument powerfully not only in *The Theory of Money and Credit* but also subsequently, in his influential book *Socialism* (in 1922), and essays on the subjective theory of value (1931) and controversies in value theory (in 1932).[5]

Having made a rigorous argument about what money is, Mises then accompanies it with a compelling argument about what it is not. Money, he says, does not allow us to make absolute measurement of an object's value. Value can only be measured subjectively, for particular individuals at particular moments in time, by observing the decisions they make.

Mises spread his arguments about the ordinal nature of utility through his influential fortnightly seminars in his office at the Chamber of Commerce. These seminars were formative (and afterwards influential) in the thought of fourth-generation Austrian economists like Friedrich Hayek, just as Böhm-Bawerk's seminar had been for the third generation (including Mises).

Oskar Morgenstern was one fourth-generation Austrian economist to be convinced by Mises's arguments about ordinal utility. Morgenstern subsequently incorporated ordinal utility into the von Neuman-Morgenstern utility theorem of which he was one of the joint creators. For Morgenstern, in a 1931 essay, individuals cannot measure utilities, but they can rank them; they can also "compare the differences...between total economic utilities by comparing them two at a time."[6] These two abilities, he argues, are all that economic actors need to behave rationally in the economy. Through the von Neuman-Morgenstern utility theorem, ordinal utility thus was incorporated into the expected utility and rational choice theory which would be the basis of mainstream academic economics after the Second World War.

That money does not measure objective value may come as a surprise to non-economist readers. For postwar economists, however, this is an important and nearly universally shared assumption.

Overlooked

Mises's contributions to modern economic thought about the nature of money, marginal utility, and business cycles are well known. Some of his ideas, such as ordinal utility, have been incorporated into the contemporary mainstream of economic thinking. Others, like his theory of the business cycle, have been remarkably influential as a counterpoint to broadly invoked ideas originating from a Keynesian perspective.

Often overlooked, though, are the extents to which Mises worked all of these ideas together into a coherent framework.

Mises was a lifelong architect of theoretical systems, both in *The Theory of Money and Credit* at the start of his scholarly career, and in his subsequent works. One example can be seen in how he links individual decision-making and price theory with his theory of the business cycle.

For Mises, fractional reserve banking leads to an inflationary spiral. Investment decisions, made on misleading signals given by excessively low rates of interest, lead to overproduction and speculative bubbles. This is the boom; the bust when it comes, as it must, takes the form of rising interest rates, destroying the illusory prosperity. However, the bust does not come from banks, says Mises. Instead, in the last phase of the business cycle, individuals choose consumption goods relative to capital goods, driving the price up of the former.[7] That is, they prefer to exchange their money (or more precisely, their supply of money substitutes, of which there is now too much) for physical things. The effect is the bursting of the bubble: and it is rooted in individual decisions about the worth of money compared to other goods.

NOTES

1   Menger, *Principles*, p. 120.

2   Ivan Moscati, "Austrian Debates on Utility Measurement from Menger to Hayek," in Robert Leeson, ed., *Hayek: A Collaborative Biography*, Part 1 (London: Palgrave Macmillan, 2013), 155.

3   Mises, *Theory of Money and Credit*, 45.

4   Mises, *Theory of Money and Credit*, 45.

5   Mises, *Socialism*, New Haven: Yale University Press ([1922] 1951). "On the Development of the Subjective Theory of Value" [1931] and "On the Development of the Subjective Theory of Value," [1932], in Mises, *Epistemological Problems of Economics*, New York: New York University Press, 1978.

6   Morgenstern, "Die drei Grundtypen der Theorie des subjektiven Wertes," in Mises and Arthur Spiethoff, eds., *Probleme der Wertlehre* (Munich and Leipzig: Duncker and Humblot, 1931).

7   Riccardo Bellofiore, "Between Wicksell and Hayek: Mises' Theory of Money and Credit Revisited," *The American Journal of Economics and Sociology*, 57/4 (October 1998), 531-78, 533.

ACHIEVEMENT

KEY POINTS

- Mises shows that it is possible to construct a wide range of political arguments from his ideas about the nature of money.

- His arguments about marginal utility and ordinal comparisons have proved broadly persuasive. Mainstream economics uses both, and even Marx's axioms have been recast to incorporate marginal utility.

- Mises extended his arguments in later works to cover topics he was unable to address in 1912.

Assessing The Argument

In *The Theory of Money and Credit*, Ludwig von Mises commences with theoretical distinctions about the precise nature of money that one reader called "seemingly arcane."[1] He then cleverly uses these distinctions to extrapolate strongly argued political insights, ranging from ideas concerning government policy about bank reserves to the business cycle.

Mises is at his best when he incorporates money into Menger's general framework of marginal-value theory. In so doing, he provides a stunningly original and intellectually satisfying way of looking at money—simply as one commodity, among many, and to which the laws of economics, including the concept of marginal utility, equally apply.

Similarly, Mises's arguments nimbly turn the tide against the view that states create money. Again, they improve greatly on Menger's arguments on the same point. In contrast, as Mises noted, "the statist

> ❝ As there are in the field of social affairs no constant relations between magnitudes, no measurement is possible and economics can never become quantitative. ❞
>
> Ludwig von Mises, *The Theory of Money and Credit*

school of German economics… probably reached its high point in Georg Friedrich Knapp's *State Theory of Money*,"[2] published in 1924.

There are some points in Mises's treatise which he revisits and revises in later works, such as his 1940 work *Nationalökonomie (National Economy)*.[3] In some of these passages, critics (including Don Patinkin*) correctly noted, Mises accidentally slipped into the sorts of circular argumentation about the value of money which he sought to correct in the work of earlier writers such as Menger.[4]

Meanwhile, Mises's criticism of quantitative social science, even as practiced by his own students, has important legacies today. With rational choice theory now firmly rooted in political science as well as economics, his trenchant criticisms of the assumptions underpinning these mathematical approaches in social science have led to a tradition of resistance warriors leveling similar criticisms today. (Donald Green* and Ian Shapiro's* influential 1996 volume *Pathologies of Rational Choice* is one example.[5])

Achievement In Context

To take just one of Mises's significant concepts and show how his contributions have shaped later economics, we might look in more detail at marginal utility.

From the time of Böhm-Bawerk on, marginal utility and the theory of value were seen as rejoinders to the challenge of Marx's own theory of value. (Many of their titles explicitly reference Marx, such as Böhm-Bawerk's 1896 *Karl Marx and the Close of his System*.[6] This is equally true of Mises, who wrote many of his works as rejoinders to socialism.)

Nonetheless, most economists, before *The Theory of Money and Credit*, assumed that utility must be some sort of quantity. After his work (and that of Vilfredo Pareto, who advanced similar arguments around the same time),[7] economics could no longer treat utility as a cardinal* quantity (that is, one measured in absolute, instead of ordinal or rank-ordered, numbers).

One result of this development has been the widespread adoption of indifference curves.* These are graphs showing different quantities of two goods, on each axis (say, cars and chocolates). Each point on the curve represents a combination of cars and chocolates which render the same utility for the individual. That is, the person has no preference for one point on the curve over any other point on the curve; every point represents an acceptable car-chocolate distribution. Furthermore, any point not on the curve could yield improved utility by being moved on to the curve. (One car may represent quite enough cars for you: a second car may carry increased insurance or parking costs, whereas a move to the curve may demonstrate you might still prefer one car and a certain number of chocolates to one car, alone.) So indifference curves capture both marginal utility and the ordinal nature of utility, which can be ranked but not measured absolutely.

While marginal utility was formulated as a rejoinder to Marx, however, economics writing in the tradition of Marx did not formulate their own response to the new thinking until analytical Marxists such as John Roemer* produced constructions of theses derived from Marx on marginalist foundations.[8]

Limitations

After he had arrived in the United States, Mises said of *The Theory of Money and Credit* that, at the time he wrote it, "I knew that we were on the eve of a great war and I wanted to complete my book before the war's outbreak."[9]

This prediction turned out to be accurate, and it meant that Mises deliberately cut short his work on the book. It would be only later, and in different works, that he would succeed in producing the more systematic elaborations of his broader ideas.

In his recollections, Mises said if he had not been as hurried, he would have started with a theory of direct exchange (that is, bartering). Instead, he decided, he would limit his scope: "in a few points only I would go beyond the narrow field of strictly monetary theory," he said. [10]

Both in *The Theory of Money and Credit*, and subsequently, Mises remained a strong critic of the mathematical turn in economics scholarship. Though this criticism was rooted in his strong views about the impossibility of measuring utility, many critics believed this represented a limitation in his thinking. Those of his students who took the further step of rendering their thought into mathematical form founded research projects which continue to dominate academic economic research today; in comparison, Mises's *The Theory of Money and Credit* can look like an elegant dead end. Duke University economic historian Bruce Caldwell* characterizes Mises, at least in the views of many economists who have worked since the middle of the twentieth century, as the "archetypal 'unscientific' economist." [11]

*The Economist** makes a similar criticism about Mises's views of the business cycle, wondering if he offers no more than a "'counsel of despair', suggesting that the authorities do nothing while a crisis blows itself out." [12] To this, Mises might well respond that, the best possible course of action might be for the authorities to do nothing, however politically unrealistic that may be.

NOTES

1   Jörg Guido Hülsmann, *Mises: The Last Knight of Liberalism,* 214.

2   Mises, *Staat, Nation und Wirtschaft* (Vienna: Manz, 1919), p. 5, footnote 3.

3   Mises, *Nationalökonomie: Theorie des Handels und Wirtschaftens.* Berlin: Buchausgabe, ([1940] 2010).

4   Don Patinkin, *Money, Interest, and Prices: An Integration of Monetary and Value Theory* (Evanston, Ill: Row, Peterson, and Co., 1956), pp 71-72.

5   Donald Green and Ian Shapiro, eds., *Pathologies of Rational Choice*, New Haven: Yale University Press, 1996.

6   Eugen Böhm-Bawerk, *Zum Abschluss des Marxschen Systems* (Karl Marx and the Close of His System), in *Staatswissenschaftliche Arbeitern: Festgaben für Karl Knies* (Berlin: Verlag O. Haring, 1896).

7   Vilfredo Pareto, *Manual of Political Economy* (Oxford: Oxford University Press, 2014).

8   John Roemer, *A General Theory of Exploitation and Class*, Cambridge, Mass.: Harvard University Press, 1982.

9   Mises, *Notes and Recollections,* Indianapolis: Liberty Fund: [1940-1], 2014, 33.

10 *Notes and Recollections,* p. 33.

11 Bruce Caldwell, *Hayek's Challenge.* Chicago: The University of Chicago Press, 2004. 125–26.

12 *The Economist,* "Taking von Mises to pieces," November 18, 2010, online at http://www.economist.com/node/17522368 (accessed December 31, 2017).

PLACE IN THE AUTHOR'S WORK

KEY POINTS

- Mises continued revisiting themes in *The Theory of Money and Credit* throughout his career, including in *Human Action*, an 881-page treatise published in 1949.

- His later work continues his commitment to free markets, and his preference for a deductive, rather than empirical, mode of research.

- Mises's postwar influence remained strong through such former pupils as Friedrich Hayek, a Nobel Prize recipient for his work on business cycles, and the link between the Austrian and Chicago Schools.

Positioning

Ludwig von Mises was 31 when he wrote *The Theory of Money and Credit* in 1912, and so he was at the beginning of a lengthy career in scholarship which would see him teaching also in Switzerland and the United States. When he retired, at age 88, he was the oldest academic still engaged in teaching at any university in the United States.[1]

Mises continued to revisit the themes in *The Theory of Money and Credit* throughout his career. One particularly definitive statement of his thought, widely considered Mises's *magnum opus*, is his 881-page *Human Action: A Treatise on Economics*, a 1949 work largely based on his 1940 German-language book *Nationalökonomie*.[2]

Human Action follows an extremely similar argumentative pattern to *The Theory of Money*, outlining one core principle and then attempting to show precisely how much can be deduced logically from it. Mises begins by discussing the concept of purposeful human

> ❝ Only by letting fall morsels of statistics is it possible for the economic theorist to maintain his prestige. ❞
> Ludwig von Mises, *The Theory of Money and Credit*

conduct. He calls the study of human action "praxeology," and argues that economics is the most developed example. In another theme that runs through his work, and in keeping with his strong commitment to classical liberalism, *Human Action* also strongly argues the case for free markets as superior to central planning.

Taken together, *The Theory of Money* and *Human Action* demonstrate Mises's preference for a deductive, not empirical, mode of research. Mises's habit of beginning with a rigorous definition of a concept and then deducing its logical consequences was heavily influenced by the thinking of Immanuel Kant,* and, in fact, Mises may be thought of as a neo-Kantian.* Such thinking is rare in a twentieth century academic landscape which became only more empirical as it progressed, and Mises's methods have attracted criticism. For example, the University of Connecticut professor Richard Langlois*—basing himself in what is, for Anglo-American economists, a more conventional perspective influenced by the philosophy of David Hume*—noted that "the post-Humean mind rebels at the hubris" of Mises deducing universally valid, empirically irrefutable truths about the human condition.

Integration

Mises's work can be considered a lifelong defense of the economics of the capitalist free market. The *New York Times*, in its obituary of him, wrote that he "was credited helping to revive respect for free-market economics in Europe," and added that "he was considered by some the intellectual godfather of the German postwar "economic miracle.""[3]

Mises's vast body of scholarship consistently argued in favor of the free market and denied that state intervention was necessary to the smooth functioning of an economy. His book *Bureaucracy*, published in 1944, insisted that the negative aspects of bureaucracy that emerged in Europe and the United States were a product of their very structures, rather than the result of ineffective policies or corruption. For Mises, government structures lack any criterion of efficiency comparable to that which acts on private enterprises.[4]

Similarly, Mises—in his largely overlooked book, *Theory and History* (1957)—weighs in on methodological and epistemological controversies concerning the writing of economic history, arguing that, because humans have freedom of will, the study of human action cannot be empirical and inductive. The situations in which action is observed, he argues, are unrepeatable.

Mises was noted throughout his career for his trenchant criticism of opponents and savage treatment of those with whom he disagreed. His aggressive style prompted one reviewer, the economist Allan Fisher, to write that "the reader sometimes begins to feel that poor old so-and-so cannot really be quite so bad as all that."[5])

Significance

In many respects, Mises and his thinking are outliers, standing apart from the direction economics took after the Second World War. Interestingly, this cleavage occurred even as mainstream economics took on board many of the arguments of his prewar scholarship, including in *Theory of Money and Credit*.

As academic economics, and indeed all social science, became increasingly mathematical and specialized, particularly in the United States, Mises continued to offer to his students and readers a cogent, carefully thought out, and reasonably consistent world outlook. He argued that mathematics was suited to physics because its subjects did not possess free will, but not to economics, which must begin from an axiom that all humans behave purposively.

This position sets Mises so far apart from the mainstream of postwar academic economics that his ideas—especially those developed after his move to America—have been taken far more seriously within the American libertarian movement than they have in university economics departments. Today, the Mises Institute, founded nine years after his death by prominent US libertarians, including Lew Rockwell* (formerly an aide for 1988 Libertarian Party* presidential candidate Ron Paul*) is one of the most important promoters of his thinking.

Nonetheless, Mises did have a strong influence on former students who continued to work within the tradition of mainstream academic economics, notably Friedrich Hayek, who continued to work on the business cycle while at the University of Chicago. As a key member in the formation of the so-called Chicago School,* Hayek also became an important link between the Austrian and Chicago Schools, the former in its prewar heyday and the latter in its highly influential postwar period. Hayek's reputation, in turn, was burnished by the award of the 1974 Nobel Memorial Prize in Economic Sciences* for his research on links between monetary expansion and the business cycle.[6]

NOTES

1   Murray Newton Rothbard, *The Essential Von Mises*. Auburn, Alabama: Ludwig von Mises Instiute, 1973, 104

2   Ludwig von Mises, *Human Action: A Treatise on Economics*, New Haven: Yale University Press, 1949. Mises, *Nationalökonomie: Theorie des Handels und Wirtschaftens*. Berlin: Buchausgabe, ([1940] 2010).

3   Leonard Silk, "Ludwig von Mises, Economist, Author and Teacher, Dies at 92," *The New York Times*, October 11, 1973, 48.

4   Mises, *Bureaucracy*, New Haven: Yale University Press, 1944.

5   Allan G. B. Fisher, "Reviewed Work: Theory and History by Ludwig von Mises," *International Affairs*, 34/4 (October 1958), 522.

6   Nobel Prize Committee, "The Prize in Economics 1974 - Press Release". October 9, 1974.

SECTION 3
IMPACT

THE FIRST RESPONSES

KEY POINTS

- *The Theory of Money and Credit* received its most favorable reviews on publication, including a positive response from the British economist John Maynard Keynes.

- Mises did not respond to criticisms of his ideas when preparing new editions in 1934 and 1953.

- His most important work, on marginal utility, was also his most widely praised and accepted contribution to the study of economics.

Criticism

When it was first published in 1912, Ludwig von Mises's *The Theory of Money and Credit* was read mainly within the Austrian School itself, and it did not attain a truly wide readership until an expanded Yale University Press edition was published in 1953.

Mises's ideas made their earliest public appearance in Eugen von Böhm-Bawerk's seminars at the University of Vienna, where (despite its criticism of Böhm-Bawerk's own arguments) the book was taught as an important set text. A rare, and chivalrous, review of the first, German, edition appeared shortly after the outbreak of the First World War in the September 1914 issue of the Royal Economic Society's *The Economic Journal*. It came from the pen of the *Journal*'s editor, none other than John Maynard Keynes.

Keynes and his followers would be lifelong opponents of Mises, differing over questions ranging from the nature of money to the desirability of government deficit spending during recessions. Nonetheless, Keynes's review is gentlemanly. He calls Mises's treatise

> **❝** The curious task of economics is to demonstrate to men how little they really know about what they imagine they can design. **❞**
>
> Friedrich Hayek, *The Fatal Conceit* (1988)

"the work of an acute and cultivated mind," says it is "not to be denied considerable merits", and admires the breadth of the field it covers and its "lucid common sense" (which Keynes adds is found so much more often in Austrian than German writers).

Keynes does weave criticisms into his courtly treatment of an enemy's work. The Austrian School, he says, was "once of great eminence, but now losing its vitality," and its veils and shortcomings "obscure the light" more than they shed it. In his treatment of the value of money, says Keynes (and this presumably includes his treatment of subjective use-value and marginal utility), Mises is "too easily satisfied with mere criticism of imperfect theories." One senses here Keynes's desire to prize Mises further away from his teachers. His criticism of Mises as "not original" presumably refers to Mises's determination to work out unsolved problems left by earlier Austrian School authors such as Menger. Yet Keynes goes on to praise Mises's efforts to relate his own theory of money to the different forms of money substitutes and inflation, saying this section "is, on the whole, the best".[1]

Responses

By the time that the 1934 English-language edition appeared, *The Theory of Money and Credit* had begun to attract a wider readership. Writing in *International Affairs*, British economist Alexander Thomas Kingdom Grant* said that its "reasoning is close and exact," though he added that "it is to be regretted… that Professor Mises has not taken the opportunity to bring the book up to date," noting that he had "ignored the more recent work of Keynes and others."[2]

The criticism that *Theory of Money and Credit* had somehow lost some of its sharp originality from 1912 grew more trenchant after the appearance of its 1953 edition. On this occasion, the economist Ralph George Hawtrey,* a close associate of Keynes, argued that the book was not only behind the times, but "cannot be said to have been fully 'up-to-date' even in 1924."[3]

Reviewing responses to Mises's work across the decades, it is difficult to escape the view that he was at his best in the vibrant, jostling atmosphere in and surrounding the university in fin-de-siècle Vienna, his thought interrogated in seminars by teachers and students who closely shared his own assumptions and who were working on related projects. Moving away from this stimulating environment, first to Geneva and then to New York, Mises seems to have gradually isolated himself and his thinking, ceasing to acknowledge the work and the ideas of his contemporaries. His subsequent work ploughs the furrows of his own thinking increasingly intricately and increasingly dogmatically, ignoring the spur of new challenges issuing from perspectives from which he might disagree.

From this perspective, it can be argued that, despite the publication of later, revised, editions, *The Theory of Money and Credit* was not only at its freshest, but also at its finest when it first appeared in 1912.

Conflict And Consensus

Most readers considered Mises's treatment of marginal utility to be *The Theory of Money and Credit*'s most important contribution, tweaking and refining the work of his Austrian School teachers on the subject until it shone. "The most important section," Ray Leffler*, an economist who taught at Dartmouth, Yale, and Michigan, called it.[4] (Interestingly, though, Keynes thought Mises's work on marginal utility to be the least original part of his treatise, seeing it as too closely based on the work of his Austrian School predecessors.)

Hawtrey, meanwhile, wondered if the very clear distinction over the origin of money which Mises draws between his own approach (in which it spontaneously arises) and Knapp's (where it is a legal creation of states) is "not so sharp as [Mises] supposes."[5] In practice, he wrote, what matters for persons receiving a medium of exchange is the knowledge they can pass it on, and use it as a medium of payment. Distant arguments about how it originated in the first place, Hawtrey suggests, are not so relevant at that point.

By 1954, even committed members of the Austrian School seemed to think of Mises as a piece of family silver dating to an era in which tastes were different. His former pupil Fritz Machlup wrote, from his post at John Hopkins University, that "some parts of Mises's treatise are definitely 'dated,'" and noted that even his new material "shows Mises as an unreconstructed sound-currency advocate." Moreover, Machlup went on to enquire whether "a young student of economics ... would appreciate just what it was that Mises contributed to the development of that knowledge." Would such a young student have to be told, Machlup mused, that "no writer before Mises" had succeeded in explaining the demand for cash using the concept of marginal utility, or his contributions to the study of the business cycle?[6]

NOTES

1   John Maynard Keynes, *The Economic Journal*, Vol. 24, No. 95 (September 1914) 417-419.

2   Alexander Grant, "Reviewed Works: The Theory of Money and Credit by Ludwig von Mises, H. E. Batson; The Problem of Credit Policy by E. F. M. Durbin," *International Affairs*, 14/6 (November-December 1935), 875-876, 876.

3   Ralph George Hawtrey, "Reviewed Work: The Theory of Money and Credit," *International Affairs*, 30/2 (April 1954). 210.

4   Ray V. Leffler, "Reviewed Work: The Theory of Money and Credit by Ludwig Von Mises," *The American Economic Review*, 25/2 (June 1935), 353-355, 354.

5   Hawtrey, 509.

6   Fritz Machlup, "Reviewed Work: The Theory of Money and Credit by Ludwig von Mises," *Econometrica*, 22/3 (July 1954), 401-402. 402.

THE EVOLVING DEBATE

KEY POINTS

- Mises's depiction of the causes of the business cycle inspired Hayek to take a similar approach. Both argue that booms are fueled by central banks allowing the money supply to grow excessively.

- For Keynes, the great problem is lack of demand, brought about by lower expected returns from new investments. Governments can "jump-start" demand by engaging in countercyclical deficit spending during recessions.

- Monetarism, which posits that central banks should encourage a slow, predictable growth in the money supply, became popular during the "stagflation" of the 1970s. The 2008 global financial crisis helped fuel the emergence of New Keynesians and New Classical Economists.

Uses And Problems

One aspect of Ludwig von Mises's *The Theory of Money and Credit* which other researchers found especially interesting, and which in fact inspired debate and contributions from very different perspectives throughout the twentieth century, was his work on the problem of the business cycle.

All economists today agree there are periodic fluctuations in employment, income, and output as nations' gross domestic product varies upwards and downwards relative to its long-term growth trend. Classical economics had attributed business cycles to external factors, such as war. For Karl Marx (who gives more attention to the point in his *Theories of Surplus Value* than in *Capital*), these alternating

> **❝** For Government, borrowing of one kind or another is nature's remedy, so to speak, for preventing business losses from being, in so severe a slump as the present one, so great as to bring production altogether to a standstill. **❞**
>
> John Maynard Keynes, *The Economy Report* (1931)

booms and busts formed part of the crises in capitalism which he believed were increasing in severity and would, in time, lead to its overthrow.[1]

Friedrich Hayek took forward Mises's own views, continuing to pursue a distinctively Austrian business cycle theory approach in his 1931 *Prices and Production*.[2] Hayek's argument is very similar to Mises's in its broad form: for him, central banks cannot possess the relevant information to properly govern the supply of money; indeed, they even lack the ability to process that information if they had it. This makes it easy for central banks to inadvertently cause a misallocation of capital by inflationary expansions of credit, says Hayek, and by excluding "the most important regulator of the market mechanism, money, from itself being regulated by the market process."[3]

Schools Of Thought

John Maynard Keynes takes a very different approach in his 1936 *General Theory of Employment, Interest and Money*.[4] For Keynes, it is not the size of the supply of money that causes booms and busts. Instead it is lack of demand, brought about by changes in the level of investment. Lower expected profits from new investments (Keynes calls this the "marginal efficiency of capital"*) cause unemployment and leave resources lying idle. During these downturns, says Keynes, governments can create demand by spending, which entices back private investment (and raises the marginal efficiency of capital).

The Great Depression ushered in an era in which Keynesian thinking dominated macroeconomics, a trend that lasted until the 1970s, when the monetarist* and "New Classical"* approaches developed by University of Chicago economist Milton Friedman* (for which he would receive the Nobel Memorial Prize in Economic Sciences in 1976) gained the upper hand in response to the severe economic dislocation that characterized that decade.

Mises's ideas—especially those regarding the value of money—can help us to understand the competing positions of these rival schools of thought. Keynes focused on the value stability of currency. He argued that panics occur when demand for money is high, but money supply is insufficient; in such circumstances, he says, government should create money to meet demand. Friedman, in contrast, argued that price stability is more important. For him, governments should foster equilibrium between supply and demand for money. They should do this by predictable, slow expansion in money supply. We can see, then, that monetarism has important similarities to Mises's and Hayek's views, even if more accepting of insights from Keynesian economics.

The contrasting approaches of the rival schools can perhaps best be seen in their analysis of the causes of the Great Depression* of the 1930s. For Keynes, the depression was ultimately the product of lack of investment. For Friedman, writing with his coauthor Anna Schwartz* in *Monetary History of the United States, 1867-1960,* it was the product of a contraction of the money supply. Inflation then took hold after the Second World War because the money supply expanded too much.[5]

Both schools have claimed success in addressing the core problems of the modern global economy over the past half century. Monetarism was influential in addressing so-called "stagflation"*—the persistent inflation coupled with slow growth experienced in the United States and Britain between 1973 and 1975. (Keynesianism, until then dominant, could neither explain this phenomenon, nor offer policy recommendations for how to combat it.) However, the followers of Keynes reasserted themselves in the wake of the 2008 financial crisis. These "New Keynesians*" argued that prices were "sticky": they do not instantaneously adjust to changes in economic conditions. In the short run, therefore, increasing the money supply (or, equivalently, decreasing the interest rate—both approaches were tried) increases output and lowers unemployment, because prices will take time to respond. The New Keynesians only suggest doing this, however, when there has been an unexpected external shock to the economy, lowering both output and inflation. Otherwise, even the members of this school have been impacted by Mises's thinking, agreeing that introducing an expansive monetary policy to effect short term gains in output and employment also increased the likelihood of inflation— and believe that eliminating this risk will prove impossible without causing a recession.

In Current Scholarship
One vibrant new scholarly field exploring business cycles is "real business-cycle theory*," which seeks to explain one of the chief concerns of macroeconomic—how and why aggregate economic activity fluctuates. It is part of the New Classical economics,* a school updating the project of neoclassical economics by building in work by Chicago School economist Robert Lucas.* Within macroeconomics, New Classical economics is a rival of the New Keynesian school.

Earlier in the twentieth century, neoclassical economics adopted the concept of marginal utility from Mises and the Austrian School. (Adding marginal utility to the tradition of classical economics as formulated by Adam Smith and David Ricardo* is what gave the neoclassical school its 'neo'.) Lucas subsequently received the Nobel Prize in 1995 for applying rational expectations* to macroeconomics and economic policy. Assuming rational expectations, in a model, means actors' expectations may be wrong but are correct over time. (They are not systematically biased, and use all relevant information in forming expectations.)

Classical economists, to the extent they thought about the business cycle at all, thought of it as a response to external (that is, exogenous*) shocks, like wars or droughts. New Classical economists take business cycles much more seriously: such fluctuations, they say, can largely be accounted for by these exogenous shocks, which represent the economy efficiently responding to them.

For real business cycle theorists (often coming from the Chicago School), shocks can include technological innovations, stricter regulation, bad weather, or changes in the oil price. These shocks change the effectiveness of capital, labor, or both, in turn altering decisions by individuals and firms about what to buy and produce.[6]

For monetarists (and Mises), business cycles happen because central banks extend money supply excessively, leading to mal-investment and speculative bubbles. For Keynesians, the case of business cycles is insufficient demand, in turn lowering the marginal utility of capital. Each school continues to have strong proponents.

NOTES

1   Karl Marx, *Theorien über den Mehrwert* (Theories of Surplus Value), *Marx-Engels Gesamtausgabe*, Section II, Parts 3.2, 3.3, and 3.4 (Berlin: Karl Dietz Verlag, [1862-1863], 1977-1979).

2   Friedrich Hayek, *Prices and Production* (Auburn, Alabama: Ludwig von Mises Institute, [1931] 2008).

3   Friedrich Hayek, *Choice in Currency* (London: Institute of Economic Affairs, 1976), 79-80.

4   John Maynard Keynes, *The General Theory of Employment, Interest and Money*, London: Palgrave Macmillan, 1936.

5   Milton Friedman and Anna Schwartz, *A Monetary History of the United States, 1867–1960*, Princeton: Princeton University Press, 1963.

6   Robert E. Lucas, Jr., "Understanding Business Cycles," *Carnegie-Rochester Conference Series on Public Policy* 5 (1977): 7–29.

MODULE 11
IMPACT AND INFLUENCE TODAY

KEY POINTS

- Mises argues that, by providing the cushion of a lender of last resort, central banks encourage inflation and free banks from the stringent discipline of the market.

- Mises's typology of money has been very influential, and two of his definitions are currently used by central banks to count aspects of the money supply.

- After the 2008 financial crisis, the US, UK, and Eurozone nations all engaged in massive quantitative easing.* Critics used Mises's arguments to warn against this.

Position

In *The Theory of Money and Capital*, Ludwig von Mises is extremely skeptical of fractional-reserve banking*, which leads to the expanding circulation in the economy of money substitutes (fiduciary media). These are only partly backed by what Mises views as actual money. The excessive expansion of money substitutes leads to destructive cycles of expansion and contraction in the economy—booms and busts.

Mises's arguments are especially relevant in examining how the world's central bankers have established a series of rules governing contemporary fractional banking, and how those rules have been applied. These global banking regulations continue to change, and are in flux at the moment.

Fractional reserve banking, and other parts of modern banking practice like the issuing of banknotes, emerged in the 17th century, particularly in London. Merchants stored their gold in private vaults

> ❝ We have had the biggest monetary stimulus that the world must have ever seen, and we still have not solved the problem of weak demand. ❞
>
> Mervyn King, former governor of the Bank of England, in a speech at the London School of Economics, January 2015.

with goldsmiths, who began lending the money out. These goldsmiths issued promissory notes* that evolved into banknotes. In 1695, the Bank of England began issuing the first banknotes. These were at first handwritten, then replaced by printed standardized ones by 1745. Fractional banking arose when banks realized depositors would not usually ask for their money at the same time, which in turn suggested that it was necessary for banks to hold liquid reserves equivalent only to some portion of their total deposits. When banks got these calculations wrong, however, the new practice could cause serious panics. For example, Britain experienced a currency crisis* in 1797, when too many worried depositors asked to withdraw their money in gold or silver (that is, in specie* or bullion*).

As a result, governments increasingly created central banks (or gave an existing bank the powers of a central bank), to issue rules about the reserves banks need to hold, and act at as a lender of last resort if any private bank faced a run on its deposits. These began with the Banque de France* in 1800, the Bank of England* after the Bank Charter Act of 1844, and the US Federal Reserve* after the Federal Reserve Act in 1913.

Most economists view central banks as an important brake on the inflationary tendencies of private banks. Mises, however, makes a provocative argument: central banking frees banks from the stringent restraints imposed on their activities by the market, and by providing the cushion of a bank of last resort, stimulates and propels banks into inflationary expansion of their loans and deposits.[1]

Interaction

In 1974, the world's ten largest central banks established a forum in Switzerland, called the Basel Committee on Banking Supervision,* to frame worldwide rules about capital adequacy:* how much money (capital) a bank should hold, compared with its liabilities.

Mises opposed all fractional reserve banking. None of these reforms have gone so far as Mises would have preferred, and imposed full reserve banking (which is to say, banking where reserves are at least equal to the sum of all liabilities). Modern reforms have only tried to limit fractional reserve banking and regulate it. In each case, the world's central bankers, gathering in Basel, have been guided by worries about risks involved in fractional reserve banking very familiar to readers of *The Theory of Money and Credit*.

The first Basel Accord (called Basel I*) was issued in 1988. Under this agreement, different bank assets were given different amounts of credit risk: cash, bullion*, and home country Treasury debt* each have no risk, while residential mortgages have 50% risk, and most business debt has 100% risk weight. Basel I says banks have to hold capital equal to eight percent of their risk-weighted assets,* which is each asset multiplied by its individual risk weight. After the global financial crisis of 2008, new requirements were released in Basel III,* further raising the amounts of capital banks have to hold (they now need to hold 27% of their liabilities in so-called "tier 1 capital"*). Even firmer banking standards were negotiated in 2016 and 2017, called Basel IV.*

Mises's insight there are different types of money has also had strong influence on how economists measure the types of money in circulation. For example, for the US Federal Reserve, M0, the narrowest measure of money supply, counts all physical currency, including coinage. M1 also includes accounts which can quickly be drawn on (like checking and current accounts). M2 (often thought of as money held by households) including savings accounts, retail funds, and small certificates of deposit.* M4 is the broadest measure, including government Treasury bills and short-term unsecured business date (called "commercial paper"*). In November 2017, there was $3.62 trillion of M1 money in circulation. Going up merely to M2, this increased to $13.79 trillion.[2]

Mises would have argued that the money supply of the United States was only $3.62 trillion. However, the fact official economists keep such close track of each type of money owes strongly to his typology in *Theory of Money and Credit*.

The Continuing Debate

Following the 2008 financial crisis, the United States, United Kingdom, and the Eurozone* engaged in quantitative easing as an unconventional way of increasing money supply. Quantitative easing, an attempt to expand the money supply and thereby stimulate economic growth (and lower unemployment) is likely where Mises's thought is now most relevant.

Mises provides arguments to be careful of excessive growth in money supply. (In fact, Mises only favors growth in the money supply when new mining deposits are discovered.) Most economists now accept his arguments that inflation occurs when money supply grows faster than the economy as a whole, reducing money's value as a medium of exchange.

Ordinarily, central banks expand money supply by lowering interest rates by buying short-term government bonds. However, this is not possible when interest rates are already at or near zero, the case for the US and Europe after 2008. To take the UK as an example, interest rates were 5.7% in July 2007, but by March 2009 had been cut to 0.5%, their lowest since the creation of the Bank of England in 1694. They remained at 0.5% or below for eight years afterwards.

Quantitative easing stimulates an economy growing at a slow rate where interest rates already are at or near zero. Here, central banks buy government debt (treasury bonds), corporate debt (bonds), and mortgage debt (mortgage-backed securities*). In the US, the Federal Reserve engaged in the first round of quantitative easing in late 2008; a second (called "QE2") in late 2010 and early 2011, while a third ("QE3" or "'QE-Infinity") stretched from late 2012 to late 2014.

Mises is a sharp critic of expansion of the money supply. However, the then-governor of the Bank of England, Mervyn King,* argued in late 2011 the money supply was actually in danger of shrinking. Quantitative easing counteracted this shrinking, said King, on the basis that "most of the money in our economy—broad money— comprises liabilities of banks in the form of bank deposits." When banks "reduce the size of their balance sheet and deleverage," he explained, "they are reducing not just the size of their assets but the size of their liabilities." That is to say, the money in circulation.

Mises's precautions were never far from their lips of opponents of quantitative easing, including the *Financial Times**, which argued central banks were trapped in a cycle of "QE-Forever," and ended by quoting Mises.[3]

NOTES

1   Murray Newton Rothbard, *The Essential Von Mises,* Auburn, Alabama: Ludwig von Mises Institute, 1973. 18.

2   Board of Governors of the Federal Reserve System, "Money Stock and Debt Measures: H.6 Release," Washington, D.C., December 28, 2017.

3   Satyajit Das, "QE-Forever Cycle Will Have an Unhappy Ending," *Financial Times*, August 1, 2016.

WHERE NEXT?

KEY POINTS

- Mises's thinking remains relevant for open questions such as understanding how to assimilate digital currencies, like Bitcoin, to conventional notions of money.

- Mises's thought offers at least two understandings of cryptocurrency: as a spontaneously traded commodity, or as a speculative bubble fuelled by central banks.

- Mises's influence in economic concepts such as marginalism and methodological individualism has spread to mainstream economics.

Future Directions

Ludwig von Mises's *The Theory of Money and Credit* continues to offer insights today, at a moment when the definition of what constitutes money is once again up for reassessment.

The advent of Bitcoin* (first released in 2009), and of other digital currencies* traded in a peer-to-peer* manner without any involvement of a central bank, throws the relationships between money, central banks, and tradable commodities into question.

Mises's book begins with a study of the nature of money, presenting the author's influential regression theorem to demonstrate money's origins as a traded commodity and hence providing one possible test for the nature and validity of the new cryptocurrencies. The questions Mises raises in this context have arguably not been so prescient, nor has money been in such potential flux, since US President Richard Nixon* ended the international convertibility of the US dollar to gold in 1971. (The link to gold was severed

> ❝No complaint is more widespread than that against 'dearness of living.'There has been no generation that has not grumbled about the 'expensive times' that it lives in. But the fact that 'everything' is becoming dearer simply means that the objective exchange value of money is falling.❞
>
> Ludwig von Mises, *The Theory of Money and Credit*

permanently in 1976.) There is a finite supply of Bitcoins: the number in existence is not expected to exceed 21 million. This restores the link between money and a tradable commodity in a way which has been absent since the 70s. Therefore, at a time when the dependence of money on the support of central banks and international financial institutions like the International Monetary Fund has never been greater, such institutions currently have no role whatsoever in digital currency.

Clearly, Bitcoin does not fit the chartalist approach of Georg Friedrich Knapp which Mises argued so strongly against in *The Theory of Money and Credit*. Knapp held that all currencies came about by a government's wish, or "fiat", Latin for "let it be done." (This in turn led to the term 'fiat currencies' to describe all money not backed up by a physical commodity, like gold.) Knapp would not have known what to make of Bitcoin.

Mises's thought, on the other hand, provides at least two ways of understanding Bitcoin. It could be understood in a similar term to the regression theorem, as an asset spontaneously used as a common medium of exchange. At the same time, investment in Bitcoin also could be viewed in terms of Mises's investigation of the business cycle, as a speculative bubble unleashed by low interest rates, and poor investment behavior brought about by quantitative easing.

Potential

Mises was drawn, more than contemporary economists in an age of academic specialism, to finding connections between different parts of a tightly connected system. *The Theory of Money and Credit* offers an example for constructing broad frameworks.

With Mises, the Austrian School finally could offer a coherent structure explaining all price and market behavior—including, thanks to Mises, money. Mises responded to Marx's challenge to classical economics, and helped show the insights of Adam Smith and David Ricardo could be recast powerfully and persuasively using methodological individualism and marginal utility.

The Theory of Money and Credit has influenced many scholars. The book's most influential concept is arguably that of marginalism; whichever economic interaction is being analyzed, the last unit added to the total determine values, cost, and revenues. Another is methodological subjectivism: viewing individuals' judgments and choices, based on information they have and consequences they expect for their actions.

Mises formulated a theory of business cycles which helped inspire one of the great research questions of economics in the century after his book was published: what causes periods of prosperity and then recessions? His own answer— excessive growth in money supply— inspired Friedrich Hayek to create one solution, the Austrian School's, to this problem, and also led indirectly to Milton Friedman's Monetarist response. His writing on the theory of marginal utility helped bring forth New Classical contributions like Robert Lucas's. Both Lucas and Friedman emerged from the postwar Chicago School, which was strongly influenced by prewar Austrian School thought.

Much of this influence manifested itself by helping to form the early thought of such notable academics as Oskar Morgenstern, Friedrich Hayek, Fritz Machlup, and Joseph Schumpeter. Hayek said of the work of Mises and the Austrian School that "the greatest success of a school is that it stops existing because its fundamental teachings have become parts of the general body of commonly accepted thought."[1]

More than other members of the Austrian School, Mises espouses political (rather than just methodological) individualism: only full economic freedom makes political and moral freedom possible, he argues. Restrictions in economic freedom lead to state coercion in politics. Political liberty and capitalist markets have been linked since both came to exist in the nineteenth century.

Mises was happy to fight for unpopular views, whether in opposing coercive redistribution, the expansion of money, credit, and government budgets, or the mathematical turn which most of his students made in the postwar period. This dedication to principle struck those who agreed and those who did not.

Summary

Ludwig von Mises is not a fashionable figure. Yet it is hard to understate the impact that *The Theory of Money and Credit*, his other 18 other books, and his 63-year-long teaching career have had on the study of economics.

Human Action has been cited by 4,687 scholarly works, according to Google Scholar.[2] Mises's student, the Princeton economist Fritz Machlup, called it a "work of truly awesome scope and intellectual range."[3] *Socialism* attracted another 1,081. *Economic Calculation in the Socialist Commonwealth,* with its argument that a centrally planned economy, lacking market prices and competition, cannot engage in rational economic calculation, drew 1,239.

The Theory of Money and Credit that has proved to be Mises's most influential work, and also his most original. Using *The Theory of Money and Credit* as a starting point, it becomes possible to trace lines of influence stretching between the Austrian and Chicago Schools, and from there to all postwar mainstream economics. Mises was a young academic when he wrote the book, but his policy recommendations and his skepticism of mathematical methods both offer ways of not only understanding, but also critiquing, the whole of the direction which the economic mainstream has taken in universities since the Second World War.

With tools honed from a study of *The Theory of Money and Credit*, a budding economics student has a conceptual toolkit to address the nature of money, microeconomic behavior of individuals describable by marginal utility—and, as an informed participant, to wade into arguments about the causes of the business cycle.

This is an exciting path that also connects the razor-sharp argument of the Austrian School, through chains of disputation and influence, to traditions as far afield in perspective as those begun by Karl Marx and John Maynard Keynes.

It is also a path still capable of yielding fresh insights and discoveries—nearly all of which can be traced back, in some form, to a seminar room in Vienna in 1912.

NOTES

1   Fritz Machlup, "Ludwig von Mises: A Scholar Who Would Not Compromise," Mises Daily Articles, Auburn, Alabama: Mises Institute. December 17, 2004.

2   Academic search engine, scholar.google.com.

3   Fritz Machlup, "Ludwig von Mises: A Scholar Who Would Not Compromise."

GLOSSARY OF TERMS

2008 global financial crisis: A global economic downturn which saw a worldwide drop in stock markets, many banks needing to be rescued by governments, increased unemployment and drops in housing markets in many parts of the world. It was the beginning of a global recession which lasted until 2012.

Akademische Gymnasium: A secondary school in Vienna dating to 1553. Gymnasien (the plural of gymnasium) are the most academic and prestigious of the three tiers of secondary schools in Germany and Austria, and the Akademische Gymnasium is the oldest gymnasium in Vienna and second oldest in Austria.

Anglo-American or **Cambridge School:** A circle of scholarship which surrounded Alfred Marshall (Professor of Political Economy at Cambridge from 1884 and often considered the father of economics as a discipline in Great Britain), along with Arthur Pigou, and Francis Edgeworth. Its projects included bringing classical concepts of supply and demand and newer ones of marginal utility and production costs into a coherent whole, by applying a greater level of mathematical rigor. (Marshall, though, did not want economics to become so heavily mathematical as to no longer be comprehensible to laymen.)

Austrian Business Cycle Theory: An economic theory, which particularly received attention from Mises and Hayek, seeking to explain business cycles as the results of an excessive supply of money, in turn the result of fractional-reserve banking or artificially low interest rates set by central banks. (This theory contrasts with the Keynesian approach, which explains business cycles as the results of a lack of demand and abnormally low marginal returns on invested capital.)

Austrian School: A tradition in economic thought which began in late 19th century Vienna and sought to apply methodological individualism to explain economic questions such as price theory. Important members included Mises, Carl Menger, Eugen Böhm von Bawerk, and Friedrich von Wieser.

Austro-Hungarian Empire: The union of the Austrian Empire and Kingdom of Hungary, governed by the Habsburg Monarchy, which existed from 1867 and ended in 1918 after the First World War.

Bank of England: The central bank of the United Kingdom, and the model on which most modern central banks were based. It was founded in 1694 and privately owned by its stockholders, then nationalized in 1946, and in 1998 became an independent public organization with guaranteed independence in setting monetary policy.

Bartering: A system of exchange in which goods and services are directly exchanged for other goods and services without use a of a medium of exchange such as money.

Basel Accords: A series of accords, of which Basel I, Basel II, and Basel III are currently in force and Basel IV is in final negotiation, which are issued as guidelines to national regulators.

Basel Committee on Banking Supervision: A committee of banking supervisory authorities established by ten central banks in 1974, which provides a forum for cooperation on banking regulation between countries.

Bitcoin: The first digital currency, released in 2009, which works without a central bank or single administrator, and instead is administered as a peer-to-peer network. Coins are produced by a process called "mining," which requires computers to solve ever more difficult mathematical problems, and hence progressively limits the rate at which new coins are released. A second key feature of the currency is that the fixed-point mathematics that underpins it caps the maximum total number of Bitcoins that can ever be produced at 21 million.

Business Cycle: The alternations in an economy of periods of economic growth (expansion or "booms") with ones of contraction (recessions or "busts"), relative to the economy's long-term growth trend.

Capital Adequacy: A measure of how much capital regulators believe a credit institution, such as a bank, should have in relation to the size of its risk taking, or liabilities.

Capitalism: An economic system based on private ownership of means of production, which are applied in pursuit of profit.

Cardinal Quantities: Cardinal numbers (one, two, three) measure the magnitude or quantity of things, while ordinal numbers (first, second, third) rank them.

Certificates of Deposit: An illiquid form of investment in which an individual gives an amount of money to a bank for a set period of time in exchange for interest, and may not take the money back until the time has elapsed.

Chartalism: A theory of money, opposed to Mises's Regression Theorem, which depicts money as originating with the decisions of states to create it.

Chicago School: A school within neoclassical economics associated with academics and former students of the University of Chicago Department of Economics. Key figures include Milton Friedman, George Stigler, Gary Becker, and Robert Lucas. Their policy prescriptions typically have included free market policies and government efforts aimed at price stability, and came under some criticism after the 2007 financial crisis.

Classical Economics: A tradition of economics often held to begin with Adam Smith's 1776 *The Wealth of Nations*, and prescribing free markets and a hands-off policy from governments.

Classical Liberalism: A political ideology which emphasizes personal, civil, and economic freedoms, together with the rule of law. Along with economic thinkers such as Adam Smith, important influences included John Locke within the British Enlightenment in the eighteenth century, and Utilitarian thinkers like Jeremy Bentham and John Stuart Mill in the nineteenth.

Commodity Fetishism: Karl Marx's idea, introduced in the first chapter of *Capital*, which describes material commodities in a capitalist society as contemporary equivalents to objects of religious devotion in earlier historical periods.

Currency Crisis: A situation in which grave doubt arises within the public whether a central bank has sufficient reserves to continue to serve as lender of last resort for credit institutions within its country, without devaluing the currency.

Digital Currencies: A currency only available in digital form and which permits instantaneous transactions, including across borders.

Diminishing Returns: A principle within economics which says there is a point when adding more of a factor of production-- extra workers at a factory, or seed on a farm field-- will produce less of a result than similar additions earlier on.

Division of Labor: A separation of tasks permitting individuals and firms to specialize in some and acquire comparative advantage.

Drohobycz: A city and district near Lviv in contemporary Ukraine, and part of the Habsburg Empire following the 1772 partition of Poland (of which it had been previously a part).

Eurozone: The monetary union of 19 of the European Union member states which have adopted the euro as common currency and legal tender.

Exogenous: External, such as a shock coming from outside a system. The opposite is endogenous, from within.

First World War: Also known as the Great War or First World War, a global war originating in Europe lasting from July 1914 to November 1918 and pitting the British Empire, Russian Empire, and French Third Republic, eventually joined by the United States, against the central European powers of Germany and Austria-Hungary. Over 18 Nine million combatants and seven million civilians died in the course of the war, which saw 70 million military personnel mobilized and new technology and industrial capacity applied in the war effort, and a protracted period of stalemated trench warfare.

The Economist **(magazine):** A weekly magazine-format newspaper edited in London which has been produced since 1843, which in its editorial line has described itself as supporting the

British Enlightenment liberalism descending from Adam Smith and David Hume.

Expected Utility: A quantity representing the returns an actor might expect from a particular course of action, corresponding to the utility that might follow from the result multiplied by the probability that it in fact will do. If purchasing a lottery ticket has a probability of n of returns of R, then the expected utility of purchasing the ticket is nR.

Fiduciary Media: In Mises's thought, the money substitutes a bank issues which are not fully backed by physical monetary units such as gold or paper money. Mises used the term *Umlaufsmittel* (means of circulation) for fiduciary media, though in some translations it is rendered as "credit".

Financial Times **(newspaper):** An English-language daily newspaper founded in 1888 and edited in London, specializing in financial and economic issues though covering a broader range of topics.

Fractional-Reserve Banking: The common practice in which a bank holds reserves (deposits) equal only to a fraction of its liabilities (including loans and investments). Bank reserves may be held either in the form of cash or in the bank's accounts with a central bank.

Galicia: A region which formed the largest, most populous, and northernmost province of the Austro-Hungarian Empire until 1918. Since 1918 has been part of Poland. It is not to be confused with the northwestern Spanish province of the same name.

Game Theory: The study of mathematical models of conflict and cooperation among rational decision-makers, using tools of equilibrium and maximized utility. It was developed in the 1940s by mathematicians, and now is being used as a leading research method in economics and across the social sciences.

German Empire: The German state which existed after the Unification of Germany in 1871, under the Hohenzollern dynasty and dominated by Prussia, until the abdication of Kaiser Wilhelm II in 1918 at the end of the First World War.

Great Depression: A severe worldwide economic depression which originated in the United States and which in most countries lasted from 1929 to 1941.

Habsburg Empire: A multinational state ruled from Vienna by members of the Austrian branch of the House of Habsburg (1521–1780) and that of Habsburg-Lorraine (1780-1918). From 1804 to 1867 it was unified as the Austrian Empire, and from 1867 to 1918 it constituted the Austro-Hungarian Empire.

Historical School (or **Kathedersozialismus**): A school of economists, based in Germany, which rejected the universal validity of economic theorems and saw economics as specific to particular situations, instead of being generalizable across space and time.

Habilitationsschrift: A thesis written, in some countries of Continental Europe, by the holder of a doctorate to permit them to teach a subject at university level. It is frequently the case that following completion of a Habilitation thesis, a junior academic would become a *Privatdozent* (men) or *Pravtdozentin* (women), as the first step in an academic career.

Indifference Curve: A series of points on a grave representing different quantities of two goods, and distributions between which a consumer is indifferent. If the axes represent guns and butter, any point on the curve represents an acceptable distribution of more or fewer guns, and more or fewer butter; a consumer at any point not on the graph could improve utility by moving to any point on the graph.

Infinite Recursion: An infinite loop in which each item depends on a preceding item, with no beginning to the series.

Inflation: Increase over time in the level of prices in an economy.

Information Society: A society where creation, use, and manipulation of information represents a significant economic and cultural activity. The term was first identified by economist Fritz Machlup in a 1962 book.

Jonathan Cape: A London publishing firm founded in 1921, taken over in 1987 by Random House, where it continues as an imprint.

Keynesian Economics: A school of economic thought that began during the Great Depression, in a 1936 book by John Maynard Keynes. Among other things, it suggests governments should engage in deficit spending during recessions, as a way of balancing the business cycle. It lost influence during the economic slowdown of the 1970s, but has had some resurgence since the financial crisis of 2007.

Labor Theory of Value: A concept applied enthusiastically by Marx, though also considered by classical economists beforehand, which explains the economic value of a good or service in terms of the average amount of socially necessary labor required in producing it. Contemporary mainstream economics instead pursued a theory of price based on supply and demand.

Libertarian: A philosophy regarding maximal freedom of choice as a key principle in economics and politics, and skeptical of the power of the state.

Libertarian Party: A minor American political party founded in 1971 to promote laissez-faire capitalism and classical liberalism. It has several representatives in state legislatures.

Logical Positivism: An intellectual movement, pursued by the Vienna Circle and Berlin Circle in the late 1920s, which propounded a theory of knowledge that said only the statements with meaning were ones which were capable of empirical verification (or, conversely, falsification).

Macroeconomics: The branch of economics dealing with national, regional, and global economies, and indicators including gross domestic product, unemployment rates, and inflation.

Mainstream Economics: Economics as currently practiced as an academic discipline in most university departments, research organizations, and government and intergovernmental bodies. At the moment, mainstream economics mainly draws on neoclassical economics (and the work of writers like Adam Smith as updated to include marginalism), while also accepting some macroeconomic findings from Keynesian economics. Other approaches, including Marxian economics and contemporary Austrian approaches, are often referred to under the umbrella term of heterodox economics.

Mal-investment: Especially in Austrian business cycle theory, badly allocated investments provoked by an artificially low cost of credit, generally the consequence of central banks pursuing an unsustainable increase in the money supply.

Marginal Cost: the extra cost of producing one more unit. Firms decide how much of a good to produce based on comparing the marginal cost with the sale price. If it is less than the sale price, the company will continue to produce it until the two are equal.

Marginal Efficiency of Capital: A term introduced by Keynes in his 1936 *General Theory of Employment, Interest, and Money*, representing the net rate of return expected from the purchase of additional capital.

Marginal Utility: The change in utility from the last one unit of input. For example, if you have five workers on an assembly line, the added product you will have from hiring a sixth. The law of diminishing returns says there is a point after which further added inputs will lead to decreasing marginal returns. Therefore, the ninety-eighth worker may not make as much a difference as the sixth.

Marginalism: A theory within economics seeking to explain differences in the values of goods and services with reference to the last unit produced or consumed.

Marginalist Revolution: The recasting of the theories of classical economics and writers such as Adam Smith in terms of marginalism, an attention to the last unit of a good or service being produced or consumed. The marginalist revolution enabled economics in the tradition of Smith to respond to many of the critiques raised by Karl Marx, and yielded neoclassical economics.

Marxian: a school of economic thought that makes use of concepts initially identified by Karl Marx* and his collaborator Friedrich Engels, which might include elements of crisis in capitalism, processes of economic evolution, and the origin of economic value. Economic work on the business cycle, as well as Joseph Schumpeter's* ideas of creative destruction, draw on the Marxian approach that market economies change over time, rather than reaching a single stable equilibrium.

Marxist: generally speaking, a person or approach quite close to the normative ideas of classical Marxism, which include giving primacy to economic analysis in explaining social change, as well as the application to politics of Karl Marx's concepts of class consciousness, alienation, and exploitation as developed in the three volumes of Das Kapital. Marxist also more often references a political orientation, where Marxian more broadly indicates any school of economic thought drawing on Marx's concepts.

Medium of Exchange: An intermediate quantity used in trades to avoid the disadvantages of a barter system, including particularly the requirement for there to be a perfect coincidence of wants.

Methodological Individualism: The requirement, promoted by the Austrian School and subsequent microeconomics, that explanations of causality in social sciences must be in terms of the preferences and rational actions of individual actors.

Microeconomics: a branch of economics that looks at individuals and firms and their decision-making.

Modeling: A representation which attempts to simplify a complex system in the actual world, by identifying several key components and formalizing these, generally using mathematical notation and concepts.

Monetarism: A school of thought largely associated with the work of Milton Friedman, which argues the objectives of monetary policy are best met by targeting a set, low growth rate of the money supply.

Mortgage-Backed Securities: A security traded on a market and which investors can purchase, backed ultimately by pooled together mortgages, particularly home loans, which are offered by the bank which issued them.

Nazism or **National Socialism:** The ideology and practices of the party which governed Germany from 1933 to 1945 under Adolf Hitler. Prominent features were racial hierarchy and racism (especially anti-Semitism) and the aim to create a racially homogeneous nation uniting all Germans living in historically German territory. In economic matters, National Socialism rejected both Marxist socialism and the free market.

Neoclassical Economics: A set of twentieth-century approaches to economics (mainly microeconomics) which builds on the tradition of classical economics which began with Adam Smith, and characterizes the work of (among others) the Chicago School. It works with assumptions that individuals have preferences over outcomes which they apply rationally, to maximize profits or utility (broadly speaking, happiness); it often assumes that all individuals have perfect information, though some approaches consider decision-making with imperfect information instead.

Neo-Kantian: A revival of the work of Immanuel Kant, which enjoyed a renewed fashionability in Germany from the 1860s onwards, prioritizing questions of knowledge (epistemology) over ones of being (ontology).

New Classical Economics: A school of thought in macroeconomics which builds on neoclassical economics, incorporating foundations in microeconomics including Robert Lucas's work on rational expectations.

New Keynesians: A school within contemporary macroeconomics which aims to provide microeconomic foundations for Keynesian macroeconomics.

Nobel Memorial Prize in Economic Sciences: An award for outstanding contributions to the field of economics, normally regarded as the field's foremost honor. The prize was established in 1968 by Sweden's central bank to mark its 300th anniversary, and though not one of the prizes which Alfred Nobel established in his 1895 will, it is referred to along with the other Nobel Prizes by the Nobel Foundation, announced at the same time, and conferred at the same award ceremony.

Numéraire: A basic standard in which value is computed. Serving as a unit of account is one of the functions of money.

Overconsumption: A situation where the price mechanism has failed to regulate supply and demand such that consumption is excessive, either through bubble economies (produced by an oversupply of credit), in terms of creating too many of a negative externality quantity (such as pollution).

Peer to Peer: A distributed form of computing which partitions tasks among a network of equal participants or peers.

Praxeology: The deductive study of human action based on the precept that humans engage in purposeful behavior.

Promissory Notes: Signed documents in which an issuer promises to pay a determined sum of money to the payee at a future time or on demand.

Quantitative Easing: An unconventional form of monetary policy used to stimulate an economy, when interests are already low, through large-scale asset purchase.

Rational Expectations: An assumption that actors within a model are assumed to know the model and take its predictions as valid.

Real Business Cycle Theory: A body of work within New Classical macroeconomics which examines whether business cycle "boom" and "bust" fluctuations may be accounted for by external shocks. These theories ask whether these fluctuations actually represent an efficient response to these shocks.

Regression Theorem: The historical argument through which Mises connects the subjective theory of value to the objective exchange value of money. According to Mises, tracing back the purchasing power of money back through time eventually leads to the point where money first emerged as a commodity traded in its own right.

Risk Weighted Assets: The amount of capital required of banks based on a percentage of their assets, weighted by risk.

Second World War: A global war lasting from 1939 to 1945, marked by over 50 million to 85 million deaths and involving 100 million people from more than 30 countries. Direct consequences included the end of European colonial rule, the start of the Cold War, and political and economic integration within Europe.

Specie (or bullion): Coins or metal money, such as of gold or silver, in mass circulation.

Speculative "Bubbles": A phenomenon when an asset trades at a price substantially exceeding its normal value. For Mises, these bubbles result from an excessive expansion of the money supply.

Stagflation: A portmanteau of stagnation and inflation referring to a situation where inflation is high but economic growth slows, with high unemployment.

Subjective Theory of Value: A theory of value set forth independently in the work of Menger, Walras, and Jevons, arguing that the value of a good is not determined by an inherent property in it or the labor necessary to produce it, but by the importance individuals place on it to achieve their own ends. Mises adopts this understanding of value from Menger; it is to be contrasted with the Labor Theory of Value.

Surplus Labor: A term used by Karl Marx in Volume 3 of *Capital*, who there argues the (normally uncompensated) labor beyond that necessary to produce a worker's own means of livelihood is the ultimate source of capitalist profits.

Tier 1 Capital: A measure of a bank's capital adequacy, referring the bank's core capital.

US Federal Reserve Bank: The central banking system of the United States, consisting of twelve regional Federal Reserve Banks created by the Federal Reserve Act of 1913.

Utility: Utility represents satisfaction, and microeconomists assume individuals will choose the behavior leading to the highest expected utility. This assumption is called rational choice. The body of work dealing with decision-making, including in conditions of uncertainty and with different tolerances for risk, is called game theory when it involves more than one actor.

Vienna Circle: A group which formed between 1924 and 1936 at the University of Vienna, of people interested in logic and mathematics, revolving largely around the figure of Friedrich Schlick, the founder of logical positivism. Vienna Circle concerns included the nature of knowledge, and the idea propositions only had meaning if they were capable of empirical falsification – that is, if they could be proved false.

Von Neumann-Morgenstern Utility Theorem: An important theorem, produced in 1947 by John von Neumann and Oskar Morgenstern, arguing rational individuals will pursue actions which maximize their expected utilities.

PEOPLE MENTIONED IN THE TEXT

Harold Batson was an assistant in the economics department of the London School of Economics and translator of the English-language 1934 Jonathan Cape edition of *Theory of Money and Credit*.

Eugene Böhm-Bawerk (1851–1914), whose full name was Eugen Böhm Ritter von Bawerk, was an Austrian economist and member of the Austrian School who served as Austria's minister of finance as well as an academic at the University of Vienna.

Bruce Caldwell (b. 1952) is an American historian of economics at Duke University, and general editor of the University of Chicago's collected works of Hayek.

Lawrence Fertig (1898–1986) was an American advertising executive and newspaper columnist who personally paid part of Mises's salary at New York University.

Milton Friedman (1912–2006) was an economist at the University of Chicago and a pivotal figure in the Chicago School, as well as an advisor to President Reagan and Prime Minister Thatcher. He was most known for his work in monetarism, arguing government should aim to keep inflation low and prices stable. He received the Nobel Prize in Economics in 1976.

Alexander Thomas Kingdom Grant (1906–1988) was an early twentieth-century economic historian in Great Britain, known for his 1937 *A Study of the Capital Market in Post-War Britain*.

Donald Green (b.1961) is an American political scientist at Columbia University and author, with Ian Shapiro, of *Pathologies of Rational Choice Theory* (1993).

Carl Grünberg (1861–1940) was a Marxist philosopher of law and history who from 1924 was director of the Institute for Social Research, and from 1911 to 1926 established and edited the *Archiv für die Geschichte des Sozialismus und der sozialen Bewegung*, an important academic journal of the time.

Yves Guyot (1843–1928) was a French economist and politician whose work offered trenchant criticisms of socialism.

Friedrich August von Hayek CH (1899–1992) was an economist whose work offered a defense of classical liberalism, and who was joint recipient of the 1974 Nobel Memorial Prize in Economic Sciences for his work on the theory of money.

Steven Horwitz (b. 1964) is an American economist within the Austrian School who currently is a professor at Ball State University in Indiana.

David Hume (1711–1776) was a Scottish historian and philosopher known especially for his empiricism and skepticism in such works as, in 1739, *A Treatise of Human Nature*.

William Stanley Jevons (1835–1882): was an English economist whose *A General Mathematical Theory of Political Economy* (1862) is regarded as one of the first important applications of mathematical method to economics.

Franz Josef I (1830-1916) was Emperor of Austria and King of Hungary from 1848 until his death, and the third longest-reigning monarch in European history. In 1867, he oversaw the transformation of the Austrian Empire into the Austro-Hungarian Empire, granting greater autonomy to Hungary.

Immanuel Kant (1724-1804) was a German philosopher who in particular argued the human mind created the structure of human experience.

Mervyn King, Baron King of Lothbury KG, GBE (b. 1948) is a British economist who served as Governor of the Bank of England between 2003 and 2013, who oversaw the Bank during the 2008 Global Financial Crisis. He entered the House of Lords as a crossbencher in 2013, and has also been, since 2014, a professor of economics and law at New York University.

John Maynard Keynes, 1st Baron Keynes, CB, FBA (1883-1946) was a British economist best known for his view that government intervention was needed to balance out "boom and bust" cycles in a nation's economy. The school of thought he founded, Keynsian economics, is the principal alternative to the Chicago School.

Georg Friedrich Knapp (1842-1926) was a German economist whose 1905 *The State Theory of Money* founded the chartalist school of monetary theory, describing money as deriving its value from its formal creation by governments.

Richard Langlois (b. 1952) is an American economist and professor at the University of Connecticut, known for his Vanishing Hand Theory.

John Law (c.1671-1729) was a Scottish economist who also served as Controller General of Finances for France, and in 1716 established the Banque Générale, which became France's first central bank. In his theoretical work he argued that money was only a means of exchange, but did not constitute wealth; nations' wealth depended on trade.

Ray V. Leffler (d.1941) was an early twentieth-century American economist who taught at Dartmouth, Yale, and Michigan and was the author of *Money and Credit* (1935).

Erik Lindahl (1891-1960) was a Swedish economist whose work involved the financing of public goods with individual benefits, a problem to which he applied the concepts of (aggregate) marginal benefit and marginal cost.

Robert E. Lucas, Jr. (b. 1937) is an American economist at the University of Chicago, and a prominent member of the approach within economics known as the Chicago School. As well as the Lucas paradox, that economic theory predicts capital should flow from wealthy countries to poor countries, he is well known for his work on rational expectations. He received the Nobel Prize in Economics in 1995.

Fritz Machlup (1902-1983) was an Austrian-born economist who lived in the United States from 1933. Among his important contributions was the concept of the information society.

Carl Menger (1840-1921) was an Austrian economist and normally considered the founder of the Austrian School of economics. One of his important contributions was the subjective theory of value, which he used to demonstrate that both sides gained in economic exchanges.

Meyer Rachmiel Edler von Mises (1800-1891) was a Vienna financier, local politician, and founder of an orphanage who was ennobled by Emperor Franz Josef I, as part of a liberalization towards the Empire's Jews. He was great-grandfather of Ludwig von Mises.

Oskar Morgenstern (1902-1977) was a German-born economist, educated at the University of Vienna and associated with Princeton University for much of his life, whose collaboration with John von Neumann yielded the von Neumann-Morgenstern utility theorem, and much of the groundwork for game theory.

Richard Nixon (1913-1994) was the 37th President of the United States from 1969 until his resignation in 1974.

Vilfredo Pareto, also **Wilfried Pareto (1848-1923)** was a Paris-born social scientist from an exiled Genoese family who assisted in developing the field of microeconomics. He was chair of political economy at the University of Lausanne in Switzerland from 1893, a position where he succeeded Léon Walras.

Don Patinkin (1922-1995) was an American monetary economist and author of *Money, Interest, and Prices* (1956). In later life he emigrated to Israel and was President of the Hebrew University of Jerusalem.

Ron Paul (b. 1935) is an American politician who represented Texas in the U.S. House of Representatives and stood as the Libertarian Party's presidential nominee in 1988.

David Ricardo (1772-1823) was a British classical economist and member of Parliament, who explored a labor theory of value as well as producing significant work on comparative advantage and on the theory of wages and profits.

John Roemer (b. 1945) is an American economist and political scientist who currently occupies the Stout chair of Political Science and Economics at Yale. He is particularly known for his work in recasting Marxian theory in terms of general equilibrium and game theory.

Claude Henri de Rouvroy, comte de Saint-Simon (1760-1825) was a French economic and political theorist and an important figure in the formation of sociology.

Moritz Schlick (1882-1936) was leader of the Vienna Circle and, as well as his contributions to logical positivism, contributed important philosophical work on the theory of relativity. He was shot and killed in 1936 by a former student who had been diagnosed previously with paranoid schizophrenia.

Gustav von Schmoller (1838-1917) was a German-born economic historian often considered the leader of the younger generation of the Historical School. He named the Austrian School in an unfavorable review of an 1883 book by Carl Menger, suggesting that its members were provincial.

Anna Schwartz (1915-2012) was an American economist and monetary scholar known for her collaboration with Milton Friedman on *A Monetary History of the United States* as well as her work at the National Bureau of Economic Research.

Ian Shapiro (b.1956) is a South African political scientist at Yale University and author, with Donald Green, of *Pathologies of Rational Choice Theory* (1993).

Adam Smith (1723-1790) is often considered the father of modern economics. A key figure in the Scottish Enlightenment, he is best known for his 1776 *The Wealth of Nations*. There he argued that in a free market, self-interested competition by individuals benefits all of society by keeping prices low, and providing incentive for a broad range of goods and services.

Marie-Espirit-Léon Walras (1834-1910) was a French economist who worked on the marginal theory of value and equilibrium theory. He, Jevons, and Menger developed theories of marginalism independently.

Max Weber (1864-1920) was a German sociologist and political economist known for such work as *The Protestant Ethic and the Spirit of Capitalism*, connecting Protestant religion with market-driven capitalism, and his model of bureaucracy

Knut Wicksell (1851-1926) was a leading Swedish economist who influenced both the Keynesian and Austrian traditions, and attempted to synthesize the works of Walras, Böhm-Bawerk, and Ricardo.

Friedrich Freiherr von Wieser (1851-1926) was an economist and member of the Austrian School (though unlike them, he rejected classical liberalism). His term Grenznutzen is the source of the term marginal utility.

WORKS CITED

Bellofiore, R. "Between Wicksell and Hayek: Mises' Theory of Money and Credit Revisited." *The American Journal of Economics and Sociology* 57 (October 1998): 531-78.

Board of Governors of the Federal Reserve System. "Money Stock and Debt Measures: H.6 Release." Washington, D.C., December 28, 2017.

Böhm-Bawerk,E. *Zum Abschluss des Marxschen Systems (Karl Marx and the Close of His System).* In *Staatswissenschaftliche Arbeitern: Festgaben für Karl Knies.* Berlin: Verlag O. Haring, 1896.

Caldwell, B. *Hayek's Challenge.* Chicago: The University of Chicago Press, 2004.

Das, S. "QE-Forever Cycle Will Have an Unhappy Ending." *Financial Times.* August 1, 2016.

Ebeling, R. "The Life and Works of Ludwig Von Mises." *The Independent Review* 13 (2008): 101.

Fisher, A. "Reviewed Work: Theory and History by Ludwig von Mises." *International Affairs* 3 (October 1958): 522.

Friedman, M and Schwartz, A. *A Monetary History of the United States, 1867– 1960.* Princeton: Princeton University Press, 1963.

Google Scholar, Academic search engine. <scholar.google.com>.

Grant, A. "Reviewed Works: The Theory of Money and Credit by Ludwig von Mises, H. E. Batson; The Problem of Credit Policy by E. F. M. Durbin." *International Affairs* 14 (November-December 1935), 875-876.

Green, D. and Shapiro, I., eds. *Pathologies of Rational Choice.* New Haven: Yale University Press, 1996.

Hawtrey, R. "Reviewed Work: The Theory of Money and Credit." *International Affairs* 30 (April 1954): 210.

Hayek, F. , *Choice in Currency.* London: Institute of Economic Affairs, 1976.

Prices and Production. Auburn, Alabama: Ludwig von Mises Institute, [1931] 2008.

The Fortunes of Liberalism: Essays on Austrian Economics and the Ideal of Freedom. Chicago: University of Chicago Press, 1992.

Horwitz, S. *Microfoundations and Macroeconomics: An Austrian Perspective.* London: Routledge, 2000.

Huerta de Soto, J. *Socialismo, Cálculo Económico y Functión Empresarial*. Madrid: Unión Editorial, 1992.

Hülsmann, J. G. *Mises: The Last Knight of Liberalism*. Ludwig von Mises Institute, 2007.

Keynes, J.M. *A Treatise of Money*. New York: Harcourt, Brace and Co., 1930.

The General Theory of Employment, Interest and Money. London: Palgrave Macmillan, 1936.

"The Theory of Money and Credit" (Review), *The Economic Journal*, 24 (1914): 417.

Knapp, G.F. *Staatliche Theorie des Geldes (State Theory of Money)*. London: Macmillan, [1905] 1924.

Leffler, R.V. "Reviewed Work: The Theory of Money and Credit by Ludwig Von Mises." *The American Economic Review* 25 (June 1935), 353-355.

Lucas, R.E. "Understanding Business Cycles." *Carnegie-Rochester Conference Series on Public Policy* 5 (1977): 7–29.

Machlup, F. "Ludwig von Mises: A Scholar Who Would Not Compromise." Mises Daily Articles, Auburn, Alabama: Mises Institute. December 17, 2004.

"Reviewed Work: The Theory of Money and Credit by Ludwig von Mises." *Econometrica* 22 (July 1954), 401-402.

Marx, K. *Theorien über den Mehrwert (Theories of Surplus Value)*, *Marx-Engels Gesamtausgabe*, Section II, Parts 3.2, 3.3, and 3.4. Berlin: Karl Dietz Verlag, [1862-1863], 1977-1979).

Menger, C. *Principles of Economics (Grundsätze der Volkswirtschaftslehre)*. New York: Free Press [1871], 1950.

Mises, L. *Bureaucracy*. New Haven: Yale University Press, 1944.

Human Action: A Treatise on Economics (Nationalökonomie: Theorie des Handelns und Wirtschaftens). Auburn, Alabama: Ludwig von Mises Institute ([1940] 1998.

Nationalökonomie: Theorie des Handels und Wirtschaftens. Berlin: Buchausgabe, ([1940] 2010).

Notes and Recollections. Indianapolis: Liberty Fund, [1940-1], 2014.

"*On the Development of the Subjective Theory of Value" [1931]* In Mises, L. *Epistemological Problems of Economics*. New York: New York University Press, 1978

Socialism. New Haven: Yale University Press ([1922] 1951).

Staat, Nation und Wirtschaft. Vienna: Manz, 1919.

The Theory of Money and Credit. Auburn, Alabama: Ludwig von Mises Institute, [1912], 2009.

Monroe, A. *Monetary Theory Before Adam Smith*. New York: August Kelley, [1923] 1966.

Morgenstern, O. "Die drei Grundtypen der Theorie des subjektiven Wertes." In L. Mises and A. Spiethoff, eds, *Probleme der Wertlehre*. Munich and Leipzig: Duncker and Humblot, 1931.

Moscati, I. "Austrian Debates on Utility Measurement from Menger to Hayek." In Leeson, R., ed., *Hayek: A Collaborative Biography, Part 1*. London: Palgrave Macmillan, 2013.

Nobel Prize Committee. "The Prize in Economics 1974 - Press Release". October 9, 1974.

Pareto, V. *Manual of Political Economy*. Oxford: Oxford University Press, 2014.

Patinkin, D. *Money, Interest, and Prices: An Integration of Monetary and Value Theory*. Evanston, Ill: Row, Peterson, and Co., 1956.

Roemer, J. *A General Theory of Exploitation and Class*. Cambridge, Mass.: Harvard University Press, 1982.

Rothbard, M.N., *The Essential Von Mises*. Auburn, Alabama: Ludwig von Mises Instiute, 1973.

Shenoy, S. R. *Towards a Theoretical Framework for British and International Economic History.* Auburn, Alabama: Ludwig von Mises Institute, 2010.

Silk, L. "Ludwig von Mises, Economist, Author and Teacher, Dies at 92." *The New York Times*, October 11, 1973, 48.

Smith, A. *An Inquiry into the Nature and Causes of the Wealth of Nations*. London: W. Strahan and T. Cadell [1776] 2017.

Steele, D. R. *From Marx to Mises: Post-Capitalist Society and the Challenge of Economic Calculation.* La Salle, Illinois: Open Court, 1992.

'Taking von Mises to Pieces." *The Economist*, November 18, 2010. http://www.economist.com/node/17522368, accessed on December 27, 2017.

THE MACAT LIBRARY
BY DISCIPLINE

The Macat Library By Discipline

AFRICANA STUDIES

Chinua Achebe's *An Image of Africa: Racism in Conrad's Heart of Darkness*
W. E. B. Du Bois's *The Souls of Black Folk*
Zora Neale Huston's *Characteristics of Negro Expression*
Martin Luther King Jr's *Why We Can't Wait*
Toni Morrison's *Playing in the Dark: Whiteness in the American Literary Imagination*

ANTHROPOLOGY

Arjun Appadurai's *Modernity at Large: Cultural Dimensions of Globalisation*
Philippe Ariès's *Centuries of Childhood*
Franz Boas's *Race, Language and Culture*
Kim Chan & Renée Mauborgne's *Blue Ocean Strategy*
Jared Diamond's *Guns, Germs & Steel: the Fate of Human Societies*
Jared Diamond's *Collapse: How Societies Choose to Fail or Survive*
E. E. Evans-Pritchard's *Witchcraft, Oracles and Magic Among the Azande*
James Ferguson's *The Anti-Politics Machine*
Clifford Geertz's *The Interpretation of Cultures*
David Graeber's *Debt: the First 5000 Years*
Karen Ho's *Liquidated: An Ethnography of Wall Street*
Geert Hofstede's *Culture's Consequences: Comparing Values, Behaviors, Institutes and Organizations across Nations*
Claude Lévi-Strauss's *Structural Anthropology*
Jay Macleod's *Ain't No Makin' It: Aspirations and Attainment in a Low-Income Neighborhood*
Saba Mahmood's *The Politics of Piety: The Islamic Revival and the Feminist Subject*
Marcel Mauss's *The Gift*

BUSINESS

Jean Lave & Etienne Wenger's *Situated Learning*
Theodore Levitt's *Marketing Myopia*
Burton G. Malkiel's *A Random Walk Down Wall Street*
Douglas McGregor's *The Human Side of Enterprise*
Michael Porter's *Competitive Strategy: Creating and Sustaining Superior Performance*
John Kotter's *Leading Change*
C. K. Prahalad & Gary Hamel's *The Core Competence of the Corporation*

CRIMINOLOGY

Michelle Alexander's *The New Jim Crow: Mass Incarceration in the Age of Colorblindness*
Michael R. Gottfredson & Travis Hirschi's *A General Theory of Crime*
Richard Herrnstein & Charles A. Murray's *The Bell Curve: Intelligence and Class Structure in American Life*
Elizabeth Loftus's *Eyewitness Testimony*
Jay Macleod's *Ain't No Makin' It: Aspirations and Attainment in a Low-Income Neighborhood*
Philip Zimbardo's *The Lucifer Effect*

ECONOMICS

Janet Abu-Lughod's *Before European Hegemony*
Ha-Joon Chang's *Kicking Away the Ladder*
David Brion Davis's *The Problem of Slavery in the Age of Revolution*
Milton Friedman's *The Role of Monetary Policy*
Milton Friedman's *Capitalism and Freedom*
David Graeber's *Debt: the First 5000 Years*
Friedrich Hayek's *The Road to Serfdom*
Karen Ho's *Liquidated: An Ethnography of Wall Street*

John Maynard Keynes's *The General Theory of Employment, Interest and Money*
Charles P. Kindleberger's *Manias, Panics and Crashes*
Robert Lucas's *Why Doesn't Capital Flow from Rich to Poor Countries?*
Burton G. Malkiel's *A Random Walk Down Wall Street*
Thomas Robert Malthus's *An Essay on the Principle of Population*
Karl Marx's *Capital*
Thomas Piketty's *Capital in the Twenty-First Century*
Amartya Sen's *Development as Freedom*
Adam Smith's *The Wealth of Nations*
Nassim Nicholas Taleb's *The Black Swan: The Impact of the Highly Improbable*
Amos Tversky's & Daniel Kahneman's *Judgment under Uncertainty: Heuristics and Biases*
Mahbub Ul Haq's *Reflections on Human Development*
Max Weber's *The Protestant Ethic and the Spirit of Capitalism*

FEMINISM AND GENDER STUDIES

Judith Butler's *Gender Trouble*
Simone De Beauvoir's *The Second Sex*
Michel Foucault's *History of Sexuality*
Betty Friedan's *The Feminine Mystique*
Saba Mahmood's *The Politics of Piety: The Islamic Revival and the Feminist Subject*
Joan Wallach Scott's *Gender and the Politics of History*
Mary Wollstonecraft's *A Vindication of the Rights of Woman*
Virginia Woolf's *A Room of One's Own*

GEOGRAPHY

The Brundtland Report's *Our Common Future*
Rachel Carson's *Silent Spring*
Charles Darwin's *On the Origin of Species*
James Ferguson's *The Anti-Politics Machine*
Jane Jacobs's *The Death and Life of Great American Cities*
James Lovelock's *Gaia: A New Look at Life on Earth*
Amartya Sen's *Development as Freedom*
Mathis Wackernagel & William Rees's *Our Ecological Footprint*

HISTORY

Janet Abu-Lughod's *Before European Hegemony*
Benedict Anderson's *Imagined Communities*
Bernard Bailyn's *The Ideological Origins of the American Revolution*
Hanna Batatu's *The Old Social Classes And The Revolutionary Movements Of Iraq*
Christopher Browning's *Ordinary Men: Reserve Police Batallion 101 and the Final Solution in Poland*
Edmund Burke's *Reflections on the Revolution in France*
William Cronon's *Nature's Metropolis: Chicago And The Great West*
Alfred W. Crosby's *The Columbian Exchange*
Hamid Dabashi's *Iran: A People Interrupted*
David Brion Davis's *The Problem of Slavery in the Age of Revolution*
Nathalie Zemon Davis's *The Return of Martin Guerre*
Jared Diamond's *Guns, Germs & Steel: the Fate of Human Societies*
Frank Dikotter's *Mao's Great Famine*
John W Dower's *War Without Mercy: Race And Power In The Pacific War*
W. E. B. Du Bois's *The Souls of Black Folk*
Richard J. Evans's *In Defence of History*
Lucien Febvre's *The Problem of Unbelief in the 16th Century*
Sheila Fitzpatrick's *Everyday Stalinism*

The Macat Library By Discipline

LITERATURE

Chinua Achebe's *An Image of Africa: Racism in Conrad's Heart of Darkness*
Roland Barthes's *Mythologies*
Homi K. Bhabha's *The Location of Culture*
Judith Butler's *Gender Trouble*
Simone De Beauvoir's *The Second Sex*
Ferdinand De Saussure's *Course in General Linguistics*
T. S. Eliot's *The Sacred Wood: Essays on Poetry and Criticism*
Zora Neale Huston's *Characteristics of Negro Expression*
Toni Morrison's *Playing in the Dark: Whiteness in the American Literary Imagination*
Edward Said's *Orientalism*
Gayatri Chakravorty Spivak's *Can the Subaltern Speak?*
Mary Wollstonecraft's *A Vindication of the Rights of Women*
Virginia Woolf's *A Room of One's Own*

PHILOSOPHY

Elizabeth Anscombe's *Modern Moral Philosophy*
Hannah Arendt's *The Human Condition*
Aristotle's *Metaphysics*
Aristotle's *Nicomachean Ethics*
Edmund Gettier's *Is Justified True Belief Knowledge?*
Georg Wilhelm Friedrich Hegel's *Phenomenology of Spirit*
David Hume's *Dialogues Concerning Natural Religion*
David Hume's *The Enquiry for Human Understanding*
Immanuel Kant's *Religion within the Boundaries of Mere Reason*
Immanuel Kant's *Critique of Pure Reason*
Søren Kierkegaard's *The Sickness Unto Death*
Søren Kierkegaard's *Fear and Trembling*
C. S. Lewis's *The Abolition of Man*
Alasdair MacIntyre's *After Virtue*
Marcus Aurelius's *Meditations*
Friedrich Nietzsche's *On the Genealogy of Morality*
Friedrich Nietzsche's *Beyond Good and Evil*
Plato's *Republic*
Plato's *Symposium*
Jean-Jacques Rousseau's *The Social Contract*
Gilbert Ryle's *The Concept of Mind*
Baruch Spinoza's *Ethics*
Sun Tzu's *The Art of War*
Ludwig Wittgenstein's *Philosophical Investigations*

POLITICS

Benedict Anderson's *Imagined Communities*
Aristotle's *Politics*
Bernard Bailyn's *The Ideological Origins of the American Revolution*
Edmund Burke's *Reflections on the Revolution in France*
John C. Calhoun's *A Disquisition on Government*
Ha-Joon Chang's *Kicking Away the Ladder*
Hamid Dabashi's *Iran: A People Interrupted*
Hamid Dabashi's *Theology of Discontent: The Ideological Foundation of the Islamic Revolution in Iran*
Robert Dahl's *Democracy and its Critics*
Robert Dahl's *Who Governs?*
David Brion Davis's *The Problem of Slavery in the Age of Revolution*

The Macat Library By Discipline

Alexis De Tocqueville's *Democracy in America*
James Ferguson's *The Anti-Politics Machine*
Frank Dikotter's *Mao's Great Famine*
Sheila Fitzpatrick's *Everyday Stalinism*
Eric Foner's *Reconstruction: America's Unfinished Revolution, 1863-1877*
Milton Friedman's *Capitalism and Freedom*
Francis Fukuyama's *The End of History and the Last Man*
John Lewis Gaddis's *We Now Know: Rethinking Cold War History*
Ernest Gellner's *Nations and Nationalism*
David Graeber's *Debt: the First 5000 Years*
Antonio Gramsci's *The Prison Notebooks*
Alexander Hamilton, John Jay & James Madison's *The Federalist Papers*
Friedrich Hayek's *The Road to Serfdom*
Christopher Hill's *The World Turned Upside Down*
Thomas Hobbes's *Leviathan*
John A. Hobson's *Imperialism: A Study*
Samuel P. Huntington's *The Clash of Civilizations and the Remaking of World Order*
Tony Judt's *Postwar: A History of Europe Since 1945*
David C. Kang's *China Rising: Peace, Power and Order in East Asia*
Paul Kennedy's *The Rise and Fall of Great Powers*
Robert Keohane's *After Hegemony*
Martin Luther King Jr.'s *Why We Can't Wait*
Henry Kissinger's *World Order: Reflections on the Character of Nations and the Course of History*
John Locke's *Two Treatises of Government*
Niccolò Machiavelli's *The Prince*
Thomas Robert Malthus's *An Essay on the Principle of Population*
Mahmood Mamdani's *Citizen and Subject: Contemporary Africa And The Legacy Of Late Colonialism*
Karl Marx's *Capital*
John Stuart Mill's *On Liberty*
John Stuart Mill's *Utilitarianism*
Hans Morgenthau's *Politics Among Nations*
Thomas Paine's *Common Sense*
Thomas Paine's *Rights of Man*
Thomas Piketty's *Capital in the Twenty-First Century*
Robert D. Putman's *Bowling Alone*
John Rawls's *Theory of Justice*
Jean-Jacques Rousseau's *The Social Contract*
Theda Skocpol's *States and Social Revolutions*
Adam Smith's *The Wealth of Nations*
Sun Tzu's *The Art of War*
Henry David Thoreau's *Civil Disobedience*
Thucydides's *The History of the Peloponnesian War*
Kenneth Waltz's *Theory of International Politics*
Max Weber's *Politics as a Vocation*
Odd Arne Westad's *The Global Cold War: Third World Interventions And The Making Of Our Times*

POSTCOLONIAL STUDIES

Roland Barthes's *Mythologies*
Frantz Fanon's *Black Skin, White Masks*
Homi K. Bhabha's *The Location of Culture*
Gustavo Gutiérrez's *A Theology of Liberation*
Edward Said's *Orientalism*
Gayatri Chakravorty Spivak's *Can the Subaltern Speak?*

PSYCHOLOGY

Gordon Allport's *The Nature of Prejudice*
Alan Baddeley & Graham Hitch's *Aggression: A Social Learning Analysis*
Albert Bandura's *Aggression: A Social Learning Analysis*
Leon Festinger's *A Theory of Cognitive Dissonance*
Sigmund Freud's *The Interpretation of Dreams*
Betty Friedan's *The Feminine Mystique*
Michael R. Gottfredson & Travis Hirschi's *A General Theory of Crime*
Eric Hoffer's *The True Believer: Thoughts on the Nature of Mass Movements*
William James's *Principles of Psychology*
Elizabeth Loftus's *Eyewitness Testimony*
A. H. Maslow's *A Theory of Human Motivation*
Stanley Milgram's *Obedience to Authority*
Steven Pinker's *The Better Angels of Our Nature*
Oliver Sacks's *The Man Who Mistook His Wife For a Hat*
Richard Thaler & Cass Sunstein's *Nudge: Improving Decisions About Health, Wealth and Happiness*
Amos Tversky's *Judgment under Uncertainty: Heuristics and Biases*
Philip Zimbardo's *The Lucifer Effect*

SCIENCE

Rachel Carson's *Silent Spring*
William Cronon's *Nature's Metropolis: Chicago And The Great West*
Alfred W. Crosby's *The Columbian Exchange*
Charles Darwin's *On the Origin of Species*
Richard Dawkin's *The Selfish Gene*
Thomas Kuhn's *The Structure of Scientific Revolutions*
Geoffrey Parker's *Global Crisis: War, Climate Change and Catastrophe in the Seventeenth Century*
Mathis Wackernagel & William Rees's *Our Ecological Footprint*

SOCIOLOGY

Michelle Alexander's *The New Jim Crow: Mass Incarceration in the Age of Colorblindness*
Gordon Allport's *The Nature of Prejudice*
Albert Bandura's *Aggression: A Social Learning Analysis*
Hanna Batatu's *The Old Social Classes And The Revolutionary Movements Of Iraq*
Ha-Joon Chang's *Kicking Away the Ladder*
W. E. B. Du Bois's *The Souls of Black Folk*
Émile Durkheim's *On Suicide*
Frantz Fanon's *Black Skin, White Masks*
Frantz Fanon's *The Wretched of the Earth*
Eric Foner's *Reconstruction: America's Unfinished Revolution, 1863-1877*
Eugene Genovese's *Roll, Jordan, Roll: The World the Slaves Made*
Jack Goldstone's *Revolution and Rebellion in the Early Modern World*
Antonio Gramsci's *The Prison Notebooks*
Richard Herrnstein & Charles A Murray's *The Bell Curve: Intelligence and Class Structure in American Life*
Eric Hoffer's *The True Believer: Thoughts on the Nature of Mass Movements*
Jane Jacobs's *The Death and Life of Great American Cities*
Robert Lucas's *Why Doesn't Capital Flow from Rich to Poor Countries?*
Jay Macleod's *Ain't No Makin' It: Aspirations and Attainment in a Low Income Neighborhood*
Elaine May's *Homeward Bound: American Families in the Cold War Era*
Douglas McGregor's *The Human Side of Enterprise*
C. Wright Mills's *The Sociological Imagination*

The Macat Library By Discipline

Thomas Piketty's *Capital in the Twenty-First Century*
Robert D. Putman's *Bowling Alone*
David Riesman's *The Lonely Crowd: A Study of the Changing American Character*
Edward Said's *Orientalism*
Joan Wallach Scott's *Gender and the Politics of History*
Theda Skocpol's *States and Social Revolutions*
Max Weber's *The Protestant Ethic and the Spirit of Capitalism*

THEOLOGY

Augustine's *Confessions*
Benedict's *Rule of St Benedict*
Gustavo Gutiérrez's *A Theology of Liberation*
Carole Hillenbrand's *The Crusades: Islamic Perspectives*
David Hume's *Dialogues Concerning Natural Religion*
Immanuel Kant's *Religion within the Boundaries of Mere Reason*
Ernst Kantorowicz's *The King's Two Bodies: A Study in Medieval Political Theology*
Søren Kierkegaard's *The Sickness Unto Death*
C. S. Lewis's *The Abolition of Man*
Saba Mahmood's *The Politics of Piety: The Islamic Revival and the Feminist Subject*
Baruch Spinoza's *Ethics*
Keith Thomas's *Religion and the Decline of Magic*

COMING SOON

Chris Argyris's *The Individual and the Organisation*
Seyla Benhabib's *The Rights of Others*
Walter Benjamin's *The Work Of Art in the Age of Mechanical Reproduction*
John Berger's *Ways of Seeing*
Pierre Bourdieu's *Outline of a Theory of Practice*
Mary Douglas's *Purity and Danger*
Roland Dworkin's *Taking Rights Seriously*
James G. March's *Exploration and Exploitation in Organisational Learning*
Ikujiro Nonaka's *A Dynamic Theory of Organizational Knowledge Creation*
Griselda Pollock's *Vision and Difference*
Amartya Sen's *Inequality Re-Examined*
Susan Sontag's *On Photography*
Yasser Tabbaa's *The Transformation of Islamic Art*
Ludwig von Mises's *Theory of Money and Credit*

Printed in the United States
by Baker & Taylor Publisher Services